Will Work for Food Family & Freedom

Still a Servant,
No Longer a Slave

By

E.A. James

FM Publishing Company
Cherokee, NC 28719

Will Work for Food, Family & Freedom
Still a Servant, No Longer a Slave

Published by:

FM Publishing Company
P.O. Box 215
Cherokee, NC 28719
United States of America
www.fasthelpministries.com

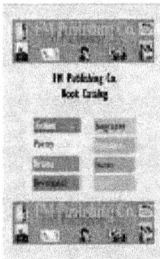

Printed in the United States of America
ISBN 9781931671064
Library of Congress Control Number 2009906474

Table of Contents

Introduction

The current economic crisis has taken a toll on so many people in the United States. Our country has filed bankruptcy so many times that the dollar will soon be as worthless as the Germany Mark was in 2002. The German Mark had been previously slated as "one of the world's most stable currencies." It was the official currency of West Germany (1948–1990) and Germany (1990–2002) until the adoption of the euro in 2002. It was first issued under Allied occupation in 1948 replacing the Reich mark, and served as the Federal Republic of Germany's official currency from its founding the following year until 1999, when the Mark was replaced by the euro; its coins and banknotes remained in circulation, defined in terms of Euros, until the introduction of euro notes and coins in early 2002. The Deutsche Mark ceased to be legal tender immediately upon the introduction of the euro—in contrast to the other Euro zone nations, where the euro and legacy currency circulated side by side for up to two months. DM coins and banknotes continued to be accepted as valid forms of payment in Germany until 28 February 2002. The Deutsche Bundesbank has guaranteed that all German mark in cash form may be changed into Euros indefinitely, and one may do so at any branch of the Bundesbank in Germany. (Wikipedia.com)

Will history repeat itself here in the United States? Euro dollars will mostly likely become the one world currency along with the formal institution of the New World Order. Life is changing as we speak and many are painfully aware that we will not recognize this country in the year 2012, that is, if we're all still here.

This book is a biographical account of my experiences in the work world after living here for over 50 years, what I've learned over those years and from those experiences, and how it has brought me to where I am now. It also takes a look at retirement, what employment really means, what employable really means, and what I believe will happen in the next coming years.

Work: A Four-Letter Word?

"Every day I get up and look through the Forbes list of the richest people in America. If I'm not there, I go to work." (Robert Orben)

Work. Who came up with this four-letter word? Well, from what I can see, it was God. In Genesis, it was pronounced upon Adam because he and Mrs. Adam, Eve, disobeyed God by listening to a snake in the grass (Satan) and eating from the Tree of the Knowledge of Good and Evil. God told Adam that by the sweat of his brow he would till the ground and then he would die. This sounds about right for most of us.

The middle class are the ones who work for 40 to 50 years, retire, and then die. The poor and indigent, that God says we will always have with us, receive public assistance, unemployment benefits, free health care, and food cards. They used to be called "food stamps," but technology move us right along. We now have electronic bank cards for this also. Of course, the poor only get just enough to die on. And, of course there are lots of rules they must follow and tons of paperwork to complete.

"Hard work never killed anybody, but why take a chance?" (Edger Bergen)

The really indigent, the homeless, skip the complicated process altogether and some prefer to rely on the generosity of people passing by the freeway to gaze upon their sorrowful faces and handwritten signs. One of my favorite cartoons is one where three men are standing outside of a cafeteria. The first two men are wearing signs "Will work for food" around their necks. The third man's sign is blank. The first man comments to the third man, *"It's not enough to just show up. You have to have a business plan."*

I remember one of the sorrowful-faced sign holders was once asked why he didn't work instead of pan handling.

He said, *"Ok, I get a job, and then what?"*

The well-dressed inquirer replied, *"You can support yourself."*

The man told him, *"I support myself now. You work, you get money, and then you use it to buy yourself a place to live, food to eat, clothes to wear, car to drive, and so on. I end up with the same thing, but mine are just not as nice as yours, because I get the throwaways."*

The inquirer was a bit disgruntled by this, and pressed the issue. *"Well, what about retirement?"*

The man replied, *"What about it?"*

"If you work for 50 years, you can retire?"

"And what will I do when I retire?"

Of course the inquirer smiled, he was about to hit home with his point. *"Ah, then you can sit back and relax, and enjoy the good life. You won't have to work for anyone else again."*

The man looked at him intently and smirked, *"Mister, I can do that now."*

* * * * *

"In fifty years, he never worked a day. To him, nine to five was odds on a horse." (Archie Bunker)

*****

Of course, like Archie Bunker, the character on *All in the Family*, most of us don't agree with the pan handler. The Bible says that a man, who does not work, should not eat. So what is work anyway? Well, according to Webster, it can be either a noun or a verb. Work, as a noun, is expressed as: labor, employment, job, vocation, occupation, effort, exertion, toil drudgery, or graft. Most of these have a negative connotation; however, work is also expressed as a: composition, design, creation, opus, masterpiece, piece, product, production, or handiwork. Work, as a verb, is expressed as "toil (to), labor (to), exert yourself, act, do, perform, affect, or bring about." When a person or a thing works, the word "work" means operate, control, drive, or run. Even with all of this, work is also expressed as "to succeed, be successful, happen as expected, or come out."

But what happens when work becomes a dirty four-letter word that spells "slavery" or "indentured servant"? Slavery in the United States was a form of un-free labor which existed as a legal institution on American soil before the founding of the United States in 1776, and remained a legal feature of American society until the passage of the Thirteenth Amendment to the United States Constitution in 1865. It had its origins with the first English colonization of North America in Virginia in 1607, although African slaves were brought to Spanish Florida as early as the 1560s.

Most slaves were black and were held by whites, although some Native Americans and free blacks also held slaves; there were a small number of white slaves as well. Slavery spread to the areas where there was good-quality soil for large plantations of high-value cash crops, such as tobacco, cotton, sugar, and coffee. The majority of slaveholders were in the southern United States, where most slaves were engaged in a work-gang system of agriculture. Such large groups of slaves were thought to work more efficiently if directed by a managerial class called overseers, usually white men. Before the widespread establishment of chattel slavery (outright ownership of the slave, and of his/her descendants), much labor was organized under a system of bonded labor known as indentured servitude. This typically lasted for several years for white and black alike. People paid with their labor for the costs of transport to the colonies. They contracted for such arrangements because of poor economies in their home countries. By the 18th century, colonial courts and legislatures had "racialized" slavery, essentially creating a caste system in which slavery applied nearly exclusively to Black Africans and people of African descent, and occasionally to Native Americans.

The previous indentured servitude was comparable to employment today. However, chattel slavery stripped Africans and Blacks of African descent of their identity, their religion, their way of life, and their homeland, and was and still is a form of genocide. Because of the lasting effects, the mutilations, lynching, rape, castration, humiliation, and other atrocities committed against a race of people whose only crime was they were made in God's (Yah's) image: they were dark-skinned people, ebony, black like Adam and Eve. They are Africans; some are the true Hebrew Israelites.

So, what happens to a people so unlike the ruling class who can no longer legally require them to work for free? Discrimination and racism. Discrimination is legal, or so I'm told. People discriminate all the time. This

9

applies in their choices and selections from milkshakes to mates. It's all right to prefer a certain flavor, style, or color when it comes to food, drink, clothes, furniture, or car. However, it becomes something altogether different when people say they have a "preference" when it comes to dating and marriage partners. The real problem comes in when people carry this preference over into the field of work and employment. I, for one, have definitely had my share.

My Life of Indentured Servitude

"I didn't have to work till I was three. But after that, I never stopped." (Martha Raye)

I've been working ever since I could remember. I grew up in Compton and we didn't have much money. However, it wasn't until I was much older and in high school that I realized my family's income was below the poverty line. I always had a roof over my head, a nice warm bed to sleep in, and enough good food to eat. However, I never owned my own bike, had to buy my own school clothes after age 13, and I never received a graduation present. I remember when my siblings and I were young, my dad used to give us quarters for A's, dimes for B's, and nickels for C's on our report cards. Most of the time I got straight A's, so eventually, the payments stopped. If we did receive an explanation, I don't remember what it was. This was my first lesson in supply and demand and economics in general.

My aunt used to pay me to baby-sit my little cousin when I was about nine or ten years old. It was easy money. A few of my neighbors used to pay me to babysit their children - again, easy money. I got to play with the kids, read stories to them, and pig out on whatever was in the refrigerator. I thought, *"It doesn't get any better than this."* I knew that you had to follow the parents' instructions carefully, make sure doors were locked and that everyone was safe, make sure you had the appropriate contact numbers in case of emergency, and treat the kids with love and respect. This was my first lesson in customer service.

My parents' favorite pastime, during my younger years, was bowling. They bowled in at least 2 to 3 leagues each week. This would become one of my favorite hangouts. Yes, I loved bowling, but I enjoyed the cash I could make keeping score for the league bowlers. I started out keeping score for my parents' team in their league. Since I was good in Math, I could add the scores rather quickly. Before long, my services were in demand. I was a happy camper. I could make $5.00 per scoring session, so I kept score for 2 to 3 leagues a day, or whenever I could. However, I never let it interfere with getting my homework done. Looking back, the education I received from the schools in Compton and Los Angeles was not the highest quality. In fact, this is an understatement. However, I read a lot, my aunt kept me challenged, and my parents bought me a Cyclo-Teacher that helped me excel in every subject – but, more about my wonderful education later.

So, there I was keeping score, giving the team members "high-fives" when they got a strike or a spare, enjoying the "camaraderie" and free food to which I was treated, and then it happened: technology replaced me. They put in automatic score keepers. Still, my parents bowled and I accompanied them. Also, around this same time, they had Blue Chip Bowling on Saturday night. People collected blue chip stamps, later green stamps. These were given away by department stores, discount stores, gas stations, and other retail outlets, as rewards and incentives to retain you as a customer. You could redeem the books for appliances, electronics, car accessories, and furniture. The more books you had, the more expensive item you could get, of course. I used to hang around the front desk where the cashier was and where the guy was who operated the manual Blue Chip counter device. People would yell to him when they had a pin setup that contained a colored pin. The pins were blue, green, yellow, and red. The red pins were worth the most. The bowling management made sure sheets were available that detailed how many stamps you would receive for each specific type of setup. You either had to get a strike to win the stamps or pick up a spare containing the colored pin. Of course, if you had all colored pins left in a spare, this was also worth a lot more stamps. I watched and I learned because it fascinated me. Little did I know this was the writer's spirit within me: we're interested in just about anything and in everything.

One day, my silent on-the-job training paid off. The guy who had been distributing the Blue Chip stamps didn't show up and I happened to be there, as usual. The manager asked me if I thought I could handle it. You better believe it! Now I'd be making $15 for only 3 hours of work, where scorekeeping afforded me the same amount in 6-8 hours. This was my first promotion. It was also my first introduction to re-training to acquire the necessary skills to meet a new workforce need. Little did I know we'd be making the change from the Industrial Age to the Information Age.

When I was 13 years old I was hired through a youth employment program to tutor English and Math during the summer at my junior high school. I was so excited, especially since these were two of my best subjects. This would become my mainstay income each summer until I reached age 15.

* * * * *

"A bum asked me 'Give me $10 till payday.' I asked 'When's payday?' He said 'I don't know, you're the one who is working!' (Henny Youngman)

* * * * *

At age 15, I was going to the 10th Grade. That summer, I had gotten a summer job working for Watts Skills Center. I would be a teacher's assistant and help tutor adults in reading, writing, math, and typing. I was nervous, but glad to help out. Just one problem, we wouldn't get paid for about a month for the first paycheck, and I needed new glasses. The glasses cost ten dollars – ten dollars, neither I nor my parents had.

We all do things we're not proud of, in fact, sometimes we try to forget them. Honesty, integrity, truth, and ethical behavior – they're just words unless we live up to them. I'd been sent to make copies of paperwork for a class. The old mimeograph machines were the name of the day back then. It was located in the teacher's lounge. One of the students was asleep on the couch. Her purse was open. When people are desperate enough and temptation presents itself, and they believe no one will find out, they sometimes succumb to the temptation. I did. I looked in her purse and found a $10 bill – just what I needed. Did I consider that maybe that was her last $10? Did I think that maybe she needed it to buy food for her children? Did I consider any of the consequences that might ensue should I be found out? Did I consider the legal, moral, or ethical implications of my actions? Sadly, I did not. I was afraid because I knew that stealing was wrong. Fear and guilt gave way to selfishness. I reasoned that she was an adult who could easily replace the $10, but I really needed new glasses. The tape around the old ones wouldn't hold the handle together much longer. So I succumbed to thievery that day.

My greatest fears came to pass: of course the woman realized the money was missing. When they investigated as to who had been in and out of the lounge area during that specific day and time, the finger pointed directly to me. The woman knew I took the money and said so. I knew I took the money. Surely everyone else knew I took the money, but I never owned up to it. Fear kept me from telling the truth. Since there was no proof, nothing was done about it. However, a guilty conscience can eat one up inside. Mine did. I got my glasses but they were bought at a greater cost to me than $10.

On the last day of the classes, to my surprise, the students in the class had taken up a collection for me. I was so ashamed and full of guilt that all I could say was, *"Well, just being here was reward enough."* My noise in my head was condemning me so loudly that I don't remember whether or not I even thanked them. I couldn't get out of there fast enough. As I left, I could see the disappointed looks on their faces. I'll never forget them. It's true that, "The goodness of God leads" us "to repentance." This would be my first lesson in the importance of employee relations and employee honesty.

As I write this, tears fill my eyes. I am overwhelmed with remorse. How could I do that to someone? I'm a different person now; this incident was close to 40 years ago. Most people would not consider it a serious incident, especially since it was so long ago. Funny, in most states, the only crimes that defy statutes of limitations are homicide, violent sexual assault, misuse of public money, and falsifying public records. My crime was committed directly against a client and indirectly against my employer and was neither of these. To those who knew I was guilty it seemed as though I got away with it. However, God, and I'm sure other individuals, knew that I'd paid for my crime with conscience and experience. It's one of the learning experiences that have shaped my behavior today, not just on the job, but in every aspect of my life.

* * * * *

"When the students are occupied, they're not juvenile delinquents. I believe that education is a capital investment." (Arlen Specter)

* * * * *

I taught my students (residents we called them) at the juvenile detention center several important lessons out of the Learning for Earning textbooks. Funny, how it wasn't until then that I actually thought about the difference between work, a job, and a career. You can work most of your life; you can hold numerous jobs; however, you have to plan for a career. A career may stem from the work you've done and the jobs you've held, but a career makes the difference between the money you make and the satisfaction and peace of mind you enjoy. Some careers require certain education and experience. I had never been taught to devise a plan, but life, the hardest teacher of all time because she gives the tests first and the lessons later, had her own plans for me.

At age 15, I was attending George Washington High School. I remember a man and a woman, who I later identified as psychologists, took me out of my English class and gave me a battery of tests. I was never told why they were testing me or for what the tests would be used. I was a shy, insecure, and timid teenager, especially when meeting people for the first time. The man who conducted the tests was kind but I was a bit suspicious of him. I'm not sure if he realized that it wasn't that I didn't know the answers to some of the questions he was asking. My social skills were undeveloped at that time, and therefore, so were my communication skills. I had not traveled very much and did not know a great deal about the world around me. I remember him asking me: *"If you were stranded in the desert in the day time, how would you tell what direction you needed to travel to find your way out?"* I told him, *"By the sun."* He asked me to explain. I couldn't. It wasn't that I didn't know. I just couldn't articulate what I wanted to say. He then repeated some 6-digit numbers, then 7-digit – all up to 10-digit numbers. At first he wanted me to repeat the numbers back to him. I did this. Then, he asked me to repeat the numbers backward. I did this. He then gave me a spelling test. I was never told that it was an IQ test. I never found out what my IQ was, but I later heard teachers and students talking about me. In my English class, someone asked how to spell something. One of the star football players (on whom I had a crush at the time) stated, *"Ask Lorraine."* I later found out that in the 10th Grade I could spell on the level of third year of college.

Shortly after this incident, one of the representatives from USC sent my parents a letter stating that I had the opportunity to go to college at the age of 15 on a special program. I wanted to take advantage of the opportunity; however, my parents felt that I wasn't ready. Also, I believe my parents would have had to come up a certain amount of money that we really did not have. Little did I know that, throughout my life, "lack of money" would continue to be a barrier to reaching my financial goals. Well, more about my wonderful student loans later. At this time, no one in my family had ever graduated from college. My mother and father grew up in families where work and jobs were emphasized more than education beyond high school. My maternal grandfather dropped out of school in the

3rd Grade; my maternal grandmother, the 6th Grade. Back then, especially for the African American race, a good job was considered more expedient than "wasting" good money and time trying to go to college.

* * * * *

"College isn't the place to go for ideas." (Helen Keller)

* * * * *

I did graduate from high school at the age of 17. Although I got straight A's in school, my SAT scores indicated that I should never attend college anywhere, anytime, anyhow. However, there were counselors who told me about opportunities opening up for minorities in the field of Biomedical Engineering. Since Science and Math were two of my best subjects, this seemed right and appropriate for me. Back then, most biomedical engineers were making six figures. I had always believed that I would either be a lawyer, a doctor, or a scientist. Since one could only reach these goals by going to college, I had always assumed I would go to college; it was only a matter of when.

I felt extremely intimidated by the University of Southern California (USC). It was an extremely large campus. There were a few minorities, but mostly Caucasians populated its illustrious halls of academia. It goes without saying that there were very few women there who looked like me. I did not have a support group, which I sorely needed. Imagine how I felt walking into my biomedical engineering class on the first day: Not only was I the only female in the class, but I was also the only African American. To make matters worse, the director of the Biomedical Engineering Department was also the professor in my biomedical engineering class. I knew I was struggling, but I needed tutoring and encouragement. I received neither. My professor called me into his office and told me, "*I really don't think you belong in that class.*" What could I say? Wasn't he the authority? Didn't he know better than I did? I was already discouraged; this statement from a man I respected was all I needed. My intention was to dropout; however, the guidance counselor suggested I take a leave of absence.

So, now I was not yet 18 but I needed a job. I got a part-time job in the evening working at Winchell's Donut House right up the street from where my parents lived. It didn't pay very much, but it was sufficient for my small needs. I met a good looking boy who conned me enough to come away with free donuts and my virginity. Eventually, I quit this job to get away from the boy and the embarrassment I felt after he bragged about "taking me down." I didn't know he had been an acquaintance of my brother.

This was a rather tough period. I didn't have a car and had to rely on the bus. However, I had no money. This was my first real experience at "pounding the pavement." It felt more like the pavement was pounding me. I searched through newspapers. Unfortunately, no Internet back then. I made phone calls. I didn't have a resume because I felt I hadn't really worked long enough on any one job for a significant amount of time. My mother would give my brother and sister rides to different places. The one time that I asked her to give me a ride she complained about us "always" wanting her to "take us somewhere." At the time I didn't realize how much stress she was under. Also, since I was the oldest, I felt more of the responsibility on my shoulders. So, I walked and walked and walked and walked. One time I walked at least 10 miles to the city of Hawthorne (we lived in Gardena) and I didn't have the strength to walk back. I called my father to come get me.

The walking did pay off. A sporting goods place wanted to hire me as cashier. I was so excited. I received very little training. Basically, they just "threw me to the wolves" and looked back to see if I survived. I was a friendly and congenial person, just like I am now. I got along with customers and with staff. There was just one problem: They started me at the end of their biweekly pay week. Since, at that time, everyone always held one paycheck in the hole, I would have to wait a whole month to get my first paycheck.

There's an age old question: which came first, the chicken or the egg? One can ask the same question when it comes to entrapment. Does the temptation come first or the innate desire? In other words, would people, who have been raised with moral values, do wrong only because the temptation and situation presents itself and they have a need? In my case, it would be too easy to say that I was "set up," but that's exactly what happened. The only thing I can think of is they knew they were hiring a young, African American woman who lived in Compton. Although I seemed nice and intelligent, they "had to be sure" I was an honest and trustworthy employee. So, what did they do in their infinite wisdom? They trapped me when I was most vulnerable. I know all too well that had the vulnerability not been present, I would not have succumbed to the temptation and would have retained my job.

Here's how the scenario went: A customer, who I'd never seen before, came into the store. He bought a fairly inexpensive item and paid for it with a twenty-dollar bill. I bagged the small item, and rang it up on the cash register. He surprised me, because before I could finish counting out his change, he promptly walked out of the store. That's the scenario. Here was my dilemma. I had no money. My father, who drove a taxicab at the time in the evening, was dropping me off at work and picking me up. He had no money to give to me either. I hadn't had any breakfast. I didn't have lunch. There was nothing to bring. I've always told people that I didn't know we were poor when I was growing up. However, I was almost grown up, and yes, I was well aware that we were poor. At the time I had no knowledge of Maslow's Hierarchy of Needs, but the bottom rung was at work that day. I was extremely hungry. When people are hungry enough, they do things they normally wouldn't. It doesn't excuse the behavior, but it does explain it.

So, I placed the cash to the side of the cash register rather than putting it into the cash register. And, get this, because this is crucial to the entire set up. When I looked around, there was absolutely no one in the store! No customers, no staff, no managers, no one. Could I have asked for a more perfect opening? Quickly, I stuffed the money into my purse. Great, I could eat. And, of course, the customer was well dressed and probably didn't need the money, or else he wouldn't have left it without a thought, right? Wrong!

The next day when I got to work, the manager called me into his office. Those words cut to the quick: "Your services will no longer be needed." I was overwhelmed with emotion that I was determined not to display. He paid me for the time that I had worked and escorted me out. As I was leaving, who did I see laughing and joking with the other employees? The customer who had come into the store and left without waiting for his change! I felt like such a schmuck. He worked there. I told my mother when she picked me up that I wouldn't be working there anymore. I'll never forget the alarm on her face when she asked me what happened. I told her they were prejudiced. She felt I was using this as an excuse, but in actuality, it was the truth. They had prejudged me. They then set up a perfect situation filled with all of the timely elements to fulfill their expectations. It was a biased test.

I hadn't been taught the lesson beforehand, but I did learn a great deal afterward. During that time, the mid 70's, there was a push for employers to hire minorities (history just keeps repeating itself, doesn't it?). So, some employers were safe in "going through the motions." I realized later that they had set me up to fail. I failed. So, now they could say, *"You see, we hired a black woman from Compton. We gave her a chance, and she stole from one of our customers. Those people just can't be trusted."* It was a self-fulfilling prophecy on their part. I was just a pawn. This was another expensive and heart-breaking lesson on employee honesty and integrity. It was also a mini lesson on office politics – a lesson I would fail many times before finally passing the test.

Sometimes your job or employment can be in other forms, preparing you for the day when you will be fully employed and receiving an actual paycheck. Such were my days in college. Didn't really think I'd actually get to college. Not everybody, especially most minorities like me, reared in low-income families, was prepared for and did well on standardized tests. However, I did get good grades in school up to and including high school. Sometimes your background and experience can count for more than just the test itself. When I graduated from junior high school, I could list certain accomplishments as receiving 8 awards, including a Gold Attendance Award.

It seems in the 9th Grade, I was the only person in the whole school to never miss a day nor be tardy for the entire three years. I'd also heard that there were 2 of us two days before the awards, but the other person was absent on that day. So, that left just me. What an honor. I was also the salutatorian and gave a speech on "congratulating the losers instead of just focusing on the winners." This has been my theme through life. The only problem with being a winner at some things – many people, out of jealousy, focused on your weaknesses and physical imperfections to make you insecure and ostracized. I was very short and little for my age, wore thick glasses, and was a shy person – a perfect target for mean, cruel, and envious peers. Well, some things never change throughout life.

In high school, I received awards in a lot of subjects, especially Science. My school counselors encouraged me and helped me to secure a 4-year scholarship to the USC in Biomedical Engineering. As stated earlier, I let fear, insecurity, and loneliness drive me away. My ex-husband was also a major player. His envy and jealousy and brutal treatment drove me away from USC. It would take 20 more years and 9 more colleges before I would receive my first degree (bachelors), but in the meantime, work was the priority.

I come from a family who has always had to work for everything they received. They didn't always value and have the time to attend and/or finish school or college. But they did work. In fact, our ancestors knew nothing else. As a slave on a plantation, you worked or you were beaten or killed. The plantation owners saw our education as dangerous and did everything in their power to circumvent it. When we were finally "free," they would then make sure our work was so hard, long, and tedious that education was still not close within our reach. When we overcame these obstacles, they made sure the quality of education was inferior. For example, I found myself re-teaching myself. I spent a lot of time in books. Since I was more of an outcast in society, I found my refuge in the library and in study. You can learn a lot this way, unfortunately, books didn't teach me about living with other people. The books I read did not teach me wisdom. I would gain this wisdom through life experience many years later and especially when studying the Bible. Little did I know God had his hand upon my life every step of the way. He allowed me to go through the trials and learn through terrible mistakes. I am a stronger person because of it, but boy did it hurt like heck.

* * * * *

"If hard work were such a wonderful thing, surely the rich would have kept it all to themselves." (Lane Kirkland)

* * * * *

After taking a year leave from USC, I went to work part-time for a company as a file clerk. This was forty years ago when a computer fit inside a huge building and companies used punch cards. Prior to this, I'd taken the test as a clerk typist to work for the federal government. It would be a while before I was offered a job. The people were nice to me. I kept mostly to myself. I was very good and quick with my hands. I was always on time and never absent. I liked what I was doing. A position opened up and they promoted me to the head of the file desk. I don't even remember if the promotion came with a raise, but I was proud of my accomplishment. I was hooked. I actually believed that if you worked hard, applied yourself, were diligent in your work, were always on time and came every day that you'd rise to the top and make the big bucks. Idealism is a wonderful thing, but reality will pop that idealistic bubble in a hurry.

I got a job offer in the mail – the Securities & Exchange Commission was requesting my services as a Clerk Typist. It was also time for me to return to USC after my year leave from school. My current employers offered me the opportunity to work part-time so that I could attend school. I remember my supervisor telling me that education was so important, that having a degree was very important. She said that if I left school then without following through it would be a very long time before I would return and finish, that is, if I finished at all. She was right. However, my parents, who never attained college degrees, saw the federal government as a great opportunity. They had never had this opportunity. The clincher was when they said, *"Now, who are you going to trust? Those people who know nothing about you, or your parents who love you and have your best interest at heart?"* Well, after that little dose of guilt, the decision was easy.

We all make choices in our lives. Everything's easier to see in hindsight, but who knows what would have been had you made different choices. When you're dealt a hand in life, you play it out the best you can until another hand presents itself. Past experience may teach you to play the new hand a different way, or sometimes you find a way to expand your options so that you have a choice in the hands you're dealt and the hands you play. Education can do this, but I would learn that a lot more than just education would be needed.

I had to catch three buses and it would take me 1-1/2 hours to get to work every day and 1-1/2 hours to get home every night, but I loved my job. Little did I know that this would be the last time I would ever use the words "love" and "job" in the same sentence.

I worked in the Law Office of the Securities & Exchange Commission. I had to work full-time, so school was dropped for now. I filed microfiche. These were little 3 x 5 plastic information records that could only be read using a microfiche reader. To me, this was technology at its greatest at that time. My boss was a flighty, gregarious Latino or Italian woman, I couldn't tell which. She was nice to me, but she did work me to death. I remember when she received all of the kudos for creating a law library. I was one who had stamped each one of those many, many law books five times with the words, "Securities & Exchange Commission." Sometimes, I typed up correspondence. I made a little more than $5,000 a year and I thought I was rich.

I had moved out of my parent's house and took a three-room apartment with a bed that came out of the wall for about $80 a month. I had no children, no one to support except myself. I was able to buy clothes every week. I was a Size 3. Life didn't get any better than that. In fact, about six months later, my boss was leaving to become an evangelist. At the time I didn't really know what that was, but from the way she talked, I knew it had something to do with preaching. I was offered a position upstairs as a typist in the Word Processing Center of the Law Offices. Wow, now I would get to see some of the documents on which the lawyers worked.

The lawyers were friendly. My boss was friendly, good-looking, and always well dressed. I hadn't worked there for two weeks until people were telling me that she was fooling around with a married man. Why they felt the need to share this information with me was beyond me, but I noted it just in case it was something I would be tested on later. There were three other women besides me and my supervisor. There we were: four Black women and one Latino woman. The Latino woman was a bit overweight, but she was one of the fastest and most diligent workers I'd ever seen. She didn't say a whole lot, but she was always nice to me. The others didn't always have nice things to say about her.

I was happy and liked going to work every day. In fact, some days I would stay later without getting paid overtime because I was so mesmerized by the new technology. They had the magnetic tapes and then came the IBM Magnetic Cards. First the IBM Mag Card I, then the IBM Mag Card II. It fascinated me that you could type a line of text, and then push a button and have it automatically repeat the line you just typed. I just had to figure out the ins and outs of the equipment. Before long, I was a whiz at it. I could churn out those law documents in no time. I couldn't understand why my co-workers were not as happy.

I remember a meeting we all had with my boss's supervisor. She was a young, slightly overweight White woman. In fact, most of my supervisors after that were either young, overweight White women or older, overweight White men. The "White" was, I felt, just part of life. The "overweight" must have been from the "good life" from all of the money they made. I remember during the meeting, my boss told her supervisor how hard we all worked for very little money. In my ignorance, I said, *"Well, it's better than nothing."* One of my co-workers, a very wise co-worker, said, *"You're absolutely right – it's better than NOTHING!"* This same co-worker told me one day, *"The more you do, the more they will expect you to do."* I found this to be very true. I would work and work and instead of paying me more or rewarding me, they just expected me to work even more.

This fact hit home when one of the White girls, who had been hired the same time as me and had the same title, received a promotion from a GS-5 to a GS-7 position. We both had the same amount of education: I had 1-1/2 years at USC; she had 1-1/2 years at UCLA. However, she could not type, but I could, very fast and very well. She went through the newspapers everyday and cut out articles for the office. I was devastated. The only variable I could find in the whole equation was that she was White instead of Black like me. I learned rather quickly that all points being equal, you will never be quite equal.

I read Alex Haley's book, *Roots*. I was mad as all get out. I loved reading biographies. I'd read the biography of Angela Davis, Malcolm X, Martin Luther King, and Cary Grant. What a contrast! Life was so very unfair. I had been treated so unfairly at the SEC. After all of my hard work, how could they do this to me? My idealism caused me to seek employment elsewhere. I quit the SEC and worked for temporary agencies as a typist. Because I could type almost 100 words a minute and I knew the IBM Mag Cards, I had no problem securing jobs. My skills were in demand. I would laugh when I remembered telling my high school typing teacher that I didn't want to take typing because I was never going to need it. Famous last words.

* * * * *

"The world is divided into people who do things–and people who get the credit." (Dwight Morrow)

* * * * *

28

I worked mornings, I worked evenings, I worked for one week, two weeks, sometimes a month assignment, but I worked. That was the important thing. Every place I worked, I learned something new. I learned a new skill and I learned a new type of computer equipment. I interacted with people who were overt racists and who were covert racists. I worked with those who were letches and those who were leaches. I worked with those who were honest and those who were dishonest. I also worked with those who were gold diggers and those who were nose diggers. I found them all interesting. I learned that I like it better not staying in one place of work too long. You bypassed all of the gossip and especially the office politics. No one feared you because you were not a permanent fixture, if there is such a thing. No matter how efficient and wonderful a worker you were, you were just passing through.

However, one can only flit through the field of work for so long before an employer snags you within its web of promises and deceit. The employer was a small privately-owned computer company. Its name was a mythical creature that I would later find to suit it to a tee: Unicorn Corporation. Everything about the place was something out of a fairy tale. I was paid a fairly good salary, but they put me in a dungeon called the Documentation Support Center. My supervisor was like an older sister who was, of course, White and overweight, but nice to me since I usually made her look good. My supervisor befriended me and did teach me a great deal. Well, by this time life had interfered with my work life. I was with my now ex-husband and had a son during my time at the computer company. Employers did not offer health insurance so I was stuck with medical bills when my ex-husband left or I left (as he or I would do repeatedly) over the course of the next 10 years. It seems throughout all of my hard work in life, bankruptcy would be my middle name. But I digress.

By this time, the IBM Magnetic Card III had come into being. In the Documentation Center, we churned out documents efficiently and effectively, for the good of the wonderful company. Of course, I was the only black person to work there. My supervisor struggled with a bad relationship and then he dumped her for a thinner and blonder woman. My supervisor's supervisor, the office manager, struggled with weekend alcoholism. I later found out that her parents made her get an abortion at the age of 13; she was then in her 50's and still couldn't forgive herself. I'm almost certain she's no longer living. I believe that had she given her life to God she would have found forgiveness in Him. During the workweek, however, she seemed fine.

The owner of the company and his wife both worked there. It was my guess they paid themselves a salary. They were always there. In fact, they micro-managed everything and everybody. You didn't question them. It seems that even when they were wrong, they were still right. I remember we had some downtime in the Documentation Center because business was slow. The owner's wife gave me a huge stack of handwritten flow charts to draw and type up. It took me a long time to do them, but I finished them. I was quite proud of myself that I'd taken on a task foreign to me but was able to complete it. I remember when I took the stack of documents to her, she said with a smirk, *"You did them, so why don't you keep them?"* It was then I'd realized she'd just given me "busy work." Some people would say, *"If that's what they want to pay me for, so be it."* I'm not one of those people.

I was only 18, but even then, I knew time was money, and I didn't like my time being wasted. I also had a great deal of integrity and I was always straightforward about things. Not everyone appreciated this trait in a person like me. In fact, I was learning rather quickly that my ingenuity and great mind would not be appreciated. I was to learn that I was viewed as a former slave with whom they had to tolerate and to whom they had to pay wages because it was the law. They could no longer force me to work for free, but they could pay me lower wages, keep me in an inferior position, and make sure my quality of life was not as great as theirs.

Eventually, the office manager left the company and my supervisor was offered the position. She politely declined the offer. She had already confided in me that she was not happy at the company and would be leaving soon. So, in my infinite naïve wisdom, I reasoned that when, and if, my supervisor left, I would be next in line for this position and would be offered the job. I did not know that my naïve personality and optimism would soon be suffering a huge blow. Since I was considered a "working supervisor," I didn't get to be a part of the "hiring committee" as my supervisor had been when they hired me. However, they did hire another individual and I became the supervisor of the Documentation Center. Still, I don't' remember if it came with any more pay, but again, I was proud of the accomplishment.

I put a great deal of processes in place and did what I could to not only streamline the processes but make sure everything was a bit more effective and efficient. So, I created a document receipt form the engineers could sign and date so that we could track whether or not we completed the job and they received it. No one seemed to have a problem with this, for a while. In the meantime, I wondered what they were doing with the office manager position. I would soon find out.

They hired a man who made no pretenses that he was a homosexual. At the time, I'd never worked with anyone who was openly gay; it unnerved me a bit, but I found him more amusing than anything else. He had a great sense of humor and wit and liked making light of most things. It's interesting how homosexuals are always trying to identify with our struggle during and after slavery and with the discrimination with which we are continually subjected. I always remember homosexuals getting jobs faster than I or anyone else could. I always remember homosexuals getting promotions and making a lot more money. Case in point: the person hired as the office manager.

Okay, so I told myself, maybe they felt I was too young for this type of responsibility, that is, office manager. I was disappointed, but I soon got over it. I consoled myself that, in time, after I've shown them how great a supervisor I can be and how diligently I can work, the office manager position would be mine one day. Wrong again! One of the first things the office manager did was hire another young White man, who was also gay, as the Office Manager Assistant. I was devastated. I couldn't believe they were doing this to me again! I did soul searching and tried to comb over everything I'd done while hired there. I tried my best to justify why they would block my upward movement this way. Again, the only variable in the equation was that I was a Black woman. At first, I couldn't discern if it was just the "Black" that bothered them or if it was the combination of the "Black" and "woman" that terrified them. I decided it was both and the fact that I was very good at what I did. Little did I realize this scenario would be a pattern that I was destined to experience until I finally had enough.

Well, despite everything, I still remained a diligent worker even though my hopes were crushed. I remember taking a document to the owner and he later stated that he never received it. The next document we delivered to him, I asked my co-worker to make sure he signed the document receipt form. While passing by the conference room a few days later, I overheard him cussing and yelling that *"...giving me a God$!%&* form to sign. Hell, if I say I didn't get the God$!%&* document, I didn't get it!* He was really angry and he stormed out of the room and saw me. I said, *"I'm leaving."* He said, *"You bet your a– you are."* I had meant that I was leaving the room. However, I decided that the company, especially the owner, didn't deserve my hard work and diligence. The office manager told my co-worker and me: *"You know, it's a shame you guys don't like J."* I gave my resignation. I didn't know the owner was suffering from cancer. He died six months after I left the company. I figured his illness was the reason he was so mean. It would seem his illness would have made him a nicer person, but he was not close to God and therefore had no peace.

I was back living at my parents' home, with a son and no money and lots of medical bills. I filed a chapter 7 bankruptcy. What a way to start off my career and work life. Funny, how you can work for years and never have anything in your life to show for it. Life is a lot different when you have children. Your choices must be made with them in mind. You cannot live just for yourself. I worked temporary jobs again and looked for another plantation on which to work. After all, I thought, all "massas" can't be the same.

My sister has had only one job her entire life, the same one she had when she was 18 years old. She's now past half a century in age. I, for one, have always admired this, but I also know that she has missed out on a lot of adventure, experience, and learning. However, I also know she missed out on a lot of the headache and trauma that I had to suffer. We are all different people and we are all wired differently. Our choices and our lives are our own. As hard as it was, I know I would have made exactly the same choices in life, just as she would. My sister worked at Northrop (now Northrop Grumman). My mom's neighbor was the Personnel Manager there. It was through these two contacts that I learned of an opening with the company. That year, I discovered that education, knowledge, skills, and experience are only a few components needed in the world of work – networking and "who you know" are crucial. They didn't help me get the position, but they did help me get an interview.

I was so happy to be working again, even though I had to take a big cut in pay. I had to take care of my son, and, it seems, my husband also. We'd gotten back together, again, and moved into a small apartment about 2 miles from my parents. My husband had odd jobs but nothing stable. When he did work, he would tell me he "lost" the money or make up some other ridiculous excuse as to why he had no money to contribute. He even took money from me. I didn't know for a long time that he was using drugs.

I came home one day from work and he, my sister, and my brother were all gathered around the coffee table with a pile of white powder. I recognized it as cocaine. I was a few months pregnant, had a son, worked all day, and I was angry. I swiped every bit of it on the floor. The looks on their faces told me that they were completed surprised and devastated. I didn't care how much they had spent and didn't care what they thought they were losing. I ordered them all out of my house, including my husband. He left with them; unfortunately, he came back.

They had a merchandise store located on the Northrop facility. I thought it was great. You could buy appliances, electronics, and furniture and have them deduct monthly payments from your paycheck. I bought a $700 stereo that I loved so much. It came up missing the next month. I'd only made one payment. My brother later confided in me that he'd seen my stereo at the drug dealer. They say drug addicts are some of the most generous people in the world: they give people your TV, your stereo, your jewelry, and your car. My husband gave away my stereo to pay for his habit. He swore up and down prior to my brother telling me what had happened, that he didn't know what happened to the stereo, and that someone must have stolen it. I was devastated. I worked so hard at that company. I only made one payment on the stereo. It was gone but I still had to make every one of those payments. This was a lesson in a great deal, especially how your social choices can impact your world of work, and how debt can keep you enslaved to a job. I remember the old rhyme, sung to the same tune the Seven Dwarfs used: "I owe, I owe, so off to work I go."

I worked for Northrop for a total of five years. During that time, I'd gotten pregnant again. I didn't like my husband very much after what he'd done to me, but I was determined that my children would be with their father because my birth father died when I was very young. He was married to someone else so I never really knew him. I'd only remembered shadows of him. I didn't get a father again until I was about nine years old. I didn't want my children to grow up without a father, but that's exactly what would happen later. My husband had sex with me while I was sleep and that's how I ended up pregnant, still having to work, and struggling and determined to be successful in my job.

It seems I have spent a lifetime having more on the ball than others with whom I worked, able to run rings around them due to my skills, qualifications, experience, and abilities, but never quite able to pinpoint for a long time why I could never quite obtain that deceptive carrot they held out just beyond my reach. Again, I worked in the Word Processing Center with engineers. They had the old Vydec machines. They were large desks that had a computer monitor and system in the middle that was part of the desk. I really liked that system. Technology just got better and better, and I loved every minute of it. I laugh when I think how much time I spent programming that system to memorize key strokes and functions that today, we accomplish by the mere push of a button or a click of a mouse. I was very good at what I did. However, I had a White co-worker with whom I worked who made it her life quest to make sure I stayed one step behind her. We were the only two in our section. She was supposed to train me. She gave me very minimal information. I learned a lot by trial and error and looking at her disks and how she created documents on the disk. I really trained myself. She was always surprised that I knew things that she hadn't taught me. When our supervisor, an older, overweight White man, told us that some of the engineers were still having documents typed by their secretaries over and over again instead of using the Word Processing Center, I made it my quest to start an in-house marketing campaign. My co-worker and I would go around and explain to them how word processing works and how much more efficient they could be my utilizing our services. My co-worker was supposed to be in charge or it, but I was the spokesperson because she didn't really have the communication and presentation skills I did. However, her presence was needed for credibility. They would listen to the "house worker" so long as the white overseer was there.

Well, our campaign worked. We increased the usage of the Word Processing Center. Who got promoted? My co-worker – to a Word Processor II. This was the first time I'd realized what my title as Word Processor I actually meant. I now understood why I had to take a pay cut after being hired there. I had no idea they hired me at a level at least 3 steps lower than what I'd been previously. I'd been a supervisor of a documentation center and they'd hired me below my abilities, qualifications, experience, and my potential. I felt so deceived. I was determined to do all I could to promote. I couldn't understand how someone like my co-worker could be promoted when she was not even good at what she did. To make matters worse, my pregnancy was causing me to feel sleepy and sick. Sometimes I had to spend 15 minutes in the bathroom and take a nap. Of course, my co-worker made sure my supervisor was aware of this and I got reprimanded. I felt that no one cared if I lived or died, and it was the truth. In other words, business is business – when it came to me.

Before long, I learned that another Word Processing Center existed with a totally different computer system. It was called the WIS (World Information System). It looked a bit more like the older PC's only bigger. They used large floppy disks like the Vydecs, but they had tape drives to back up the information every day. I was moved into this center with two Black females, my previous White co-worker, and another White female. My lead was an older, overweight White woman. She seemed kind enough but there was something sinister about her that lay underneath that I couldn't quite put my finger on.

I learned a great deal in that place. I learned how to create user accounts and backup the tape drives. I learned how to create even more documents and the ins and outs of the WIS. I also learned that co-workers can be devious and cruel due to their jealousy and envy. I was a lot faster than my co-workers because I was good at what I did. I didn't sit around all day and gossip like some of them. I did my work. I remember completing my assignments for the day and left my disks on the table for my lead. The next day, the two White females were snickering when my supervisor told me that the disks I'd left didn't have anything on them. I told him that just couldn't be. The lead told me in front of my supervisor that perhaps I should slow down so I wouldn't make so many mistakes. I thought, "What mistakes?" I had a pretty good memory for things. I know I'd completed everything. How could I have erased the documents? I had been too trusting. That was the first time I realized people were always going to make sure I didn't rise any higher than they did. It reminded me of the crabs in a barrel. As soon as one of them starts crawling to the top to possibly get out of the barrel, the others jump up and pull the ambitious crab back down. I just had to get out of that barrel.

Well, my first co-worker that had been previously promoted was promoted again. She was now a Word Processor III. However, I too got promoted to a Word Processor II. Time went on and I went out on maternity leave. It was great to be off for the six months. I could breast feed my daughter like I'd done with my son but I now had medical benefits. They weren't the greatest, but they were good enough. I loved my children. They were the light of my life, despite what my husband put me through. I eventually rented a house that was supposed to be with an option to buy, but I later discovered the woman was just trying to get her husband out of her life. It was a big 4-bedroom house with a huge backyard in Compton where I grew up. My husband never gave me any help so after several attempts having him live with me, I finally asked him to leave. When I went back to work, I was leaving my children at a day care. I loved my children, but sometimes one had to go to work to get away from them. Single parents were never meant to be. God did not ordain it that way. Our faults, imperfections, and disobedience get in the way and we make our lives harder than what they really have to be. Yes, this would be my theme song for a while.

This time it was my White co-worker's turn to be pregnant. The difference: she had a husband who was right there with her. She had the other White co-worker who covered for her when she took an hour nap in the bathroom. She had been promoted to Word Processor Specialist just weeks prior to her pregnancy. When she went out on maternity leave, they asked me to do her job, without a promotion. By now, I had gained a small bit of wisdom and knew that this part of the deal was negotiable. I told my supervisor that unless I was promoted to the Word Processor Specialist position, I would just sit in my little cubby hole, do my job, and nothing more. I got the promotion. I was moved in the area where my supervisor was. I got to meet the rest of the group in the engineering department. There was an Italian woman who I thought was very friendly and 8 other White male engineers. I was a Size 4 and wore tight skirts. I thought I was quite good-looking back then once I'd replaced my glasses with contacts. My self-esteem greatly improved. I had a great sense of humor, could imitate Mae West, and told raunchy jokes to amuse my co-workers. I was the stereotypical "Sapphire." At the time I thought I was just having fun at work. I was so young, so ignorant, and so un-saved. I met my friends Michael and Anna during that time. They both worked at Northrop. Michael was a Christian. He was such a sweet, patient, and mild-mannered person. I adored him as a friend. I remember him witnessing to me. I had been baptized at 9, but didn't really know the Lord. He started telling me about Hell. I told him, *"I'm not worried about going to Hell, because when I get to Hell I'll be so busy shaking hands with old friends, I won't have time to worry."* I really didn't have a clue back then. Sin had clouded my spiritual understanding. One thing about God – he is the all knowing, ever-present, all powerful, expert fisherman. Once he has hooked you, he'll give you a bit of line and even allow you to swim away if you choose to, but bit by bit, he'll reel you back in. Little did I know I was about to feel my first big tug on that gospel line.

Being promoted, I worked even harder. I'm not sure if it was something inside that felt I had to "prove" I was worthy of the promotion. I was now a Word Processing Specialist and supervised several of the other girls in the Word Processing Center. My life took several downturns. Back then, sexual harassment was not a hot topic and something women went to court over. You experienced it, you suffered in silence, or you usually quit your job and looked for another one. I'm sure it's because of my provocative dress and sexual prowess that I experienced what I did, but it disappointed me that I was treated this way. The first time was when one of the White engineers (as they all were then except for one) made me think he was interested in me. He and the other two engineers were friendly to me, and I to them. I would usually deliver their documents to them and stand and chat a few minutes. Little did I know that they would take turns getting my attention so the others could ogle my buttocks. Then one day, the one I thought could possibly marry me, after dating of course, made a move on me by putting his fingers up through and underneath my skirt. It happened so fast that I couldn't believe he'd done it. He had this smug and pleased look on his face. He was actually delighted in the surprised look on my face. I was devastated. I stayed clear of him after that. Eventually, he transferred to another section. I saw him one day in the cafeteria affectionately talking with a White older heavyset female.

The next time came way out of left field. I had to work overtime to help my boss with some paperwork. He'd requested that I stay later. I had to call the babysitter and tell her I'd be late. I noticed that when he was talking with me he would get too close for comfort. There was no one else around. I didn't think much of it at first but I kept remembering the time I was raped when I was 18. I didn't report it, nor did I tell anyone until 10 years after. I was not hurt, just scared out of my wits and humiliated beyond what a person should have to endure. But my mother raised a strong person, but like I said, wisdom came very slowly. My boss's advances made me feel very uncomfortable, so I told him I was not feeling well and needed to leave earlier than I'd promised to work. He got the hint and never bothered me again.

Throughout my life, I've always felt that "Mr. Right" was out there somewhere. However, I now know that the only Mr. Right is Jesus Christ. When God gives you a husband, he will always be the right one. I remember they hired several young Black engineers in a department to which I would delivered documents that were typed. Now we had two of them – one young and one older. One of them I thought was attractive. My friend Anna and I used to discuss him. I decided to hand him a paper with my name and phone number on it. He gladly accepted it and told me it was "refreshing" for a woman to be the one to make the first move. However, it was not long after that I realized, through his candid verbal remarks, he was only interested in having sex and a one-night stand. I used to make silly sexual innuendo jokes, but he was lewd and crass. I didn't realize that sexual harassment could also be verbal, but I found out soon enough.

The next encounter almost cost me my life. It was only because of the grace of God that I'm alive to write about it. My mother used to always tell me, *"God takes care of babies and fools, and you're not a baby anymore."* This is one former fool that is extremely grateful for God's mercy. One of the White engineers who I'd never seen before came up to me and asked me if I'd like to have dinner with him some evening. He seemed friendly, but the sign he had on his cubicle bothered me. It said: *"Life's a [b-word], and then you die."* I thought, my life's not that great, but it's still worth living. Did he think that was all we had to look forward to? He said he was recently divorced, had moved into his own house, and needed someone to help him decorate and fix things up. He said he needed a "woman's perspective." Until this day I know that interior decorating is not one of my gifts; however, I do have a gift of compassion and love for others. My compassion and love for others wanted to help him and said, "Yes, I will." However, after much silent contemplation about the situation, and I know it was God's prompting, my common sense won out. I didn't tell him I wasn't coming. I just didn't show up.

He didn't show up for work the next few days. It would be a week later that they were all discussing what had happened to him. Apparently, he'd had a great deal of debt and went bankrupt. His wife left him and took their children. They found him dead in his house. He'd committed suicide. He shot himself in the mouth. Right then and there I realized he could have taken me with him. People in that state of mind usually want company with whom to die. I didn't know until then that God allowed me to experience these things to nudge me back toward him. But, apparently, God was not finished yet. The field of work would continue to torture me.

I made so many bad decisions. My children suffered behind it. The unthinkable had happened. Someone I trusted, a man with whom I lived, molested both of my son and daughter. He had begged me to move in after his guardian father passed away that Christmas. His guardian mother lived with him. She was very elderly. However, he had suggested that I let her babysit. After all, he would be there. He only had one lung so he was out on permanent disability. I didn't know until after the fact that he only had one lung because he'd smoked PCP most of his life. I won't give too much space to this topic because this book is about the field of work; so, to make a long story short, this man whom I entrusted the care of my children and my heart, tore my heart to shreds. He molested my children. The problem: he swore up and down he didn't do anything. I didn't want to get the police involved. If I wanted the police involved in my life, I would have reported my rape years ago. I had decided to try to move back in with my parents. However, I was received with a polite "no" and reasons why. I had decided to place my children back into the care of their former babysitter. In the meantime, I informed my boyfriend's step-mother. She and he got into an altercation. She reported the abuse to the police, we were taken to the hospital where the molestation was confirmed. I was charged with neglect. How those words "neglect" seared my innermost being. Neglect? My ex-husband never took time to help me with my children. He never paid child support. They had the wrong parent. It was later that God would show me that according to man's laws, I wasn't really guilty of neglect. However, according to His laws, I *was* guilty of neglect because I hadn't given my children Him. How could I? I wasn't serving Him myself.

They took my children from me for a total of six agonizing, painstaking months. I jumped through hoops and did whatever I needed to regain custody of my children. It was through the faith and prayers of my aunts that I came through victoriously. I didn't ask God for a Black female judge, but that's exactly what he sent. I'd written a rebuttal to the court and explained everything. They had tried to make me out to be a terrible and awful, neglectful parent. However, the evidence didn't justify it. All those months I still went to work. I'd changed a great deal, but I worked. This was all I had for a long while. However, I regained custody of my children. I moved into my own place. I was offered an apartment by one of the Black engineers who I knew liked me. I rented it. He also sold to me, at a very reasonable price, a good running older model Buick. I'd heard talk around the office that he and I would be getting together.

My friend Keith had other plans. Not sure where he'd come from. When I think back, I guess he'd always been there, but just never talked to me. We had an instant magnetism. I couldn't explain it. We looked so different, came from different families with totally different backgrounds. We were both educated; however, he had a degree and I didn't at the time. Anyway, he and I started dating. From experience, I believe it's not a good idea to date someone with whom you work. It saves a lot of heartache and trouble. However, Keith and I were fine. The rest of the people had a serious problem with our relationship. It just didn't look right. How could I pass up the Black engineer, who's first initial also happened to be a "K," for a White engineer who was two years younger than me? Come to think of it, Keith was kind of strange. He was a vegetarian and passed gas silently on a repeated basis. But I loved him. He was kind, smart, adventurous, and taught me so many things. The Black engineer told me, *"They're going to get both of you for getting together."* I'm not sure if the Black engineer meant well or if he said what he said out of jealously, either way he was right.

Racial discrimination. What a terrible phrase. Funny, how it rolls easily off the tongue, but leaves a sinking feeling in the pit of the stomach. For anyone who's ever encountered it (and it seems I would encounter it repeatedly), they know it's like being raped over and over again. You have to trust again, because you still have to work. Many court cases have come before well-meaning judges accusing defendants of age discrimination, sex discrimination, and discrimination against someone with a disability. These three, especially the latter, appear to be easily proved. However, racial discrimination was not easily proved, especially when you came up against a big company like Northrop back in the

80's. I would learn that you need at least one or two other people who had experienced the same thing and who were brave enough to testify to it. Otherwise, you didn't have a case. Some lessons are hard learned.

No one likes going up against the company that they work for. I'm sure a person doesn't wake up one day and say, *"Gee, I guess I'll file charges against them with the EEOC."* It's extremely uncomfortable and almost a no-win situation for everyone. Only if you truly believe you are right and have in fact been discriminated against due to your race, should you even consider it, and even then... The scenario went something like this: my co-worker, who had gone out on maternity leave, was now back at work, in full swing, and extremely resentful that I was in the same position as she was. So, here they had two Word Processing Specialists. The older White heavyset woman had retired. I believe the trauma she'd experienced due to accidentally running down a person who just wandered out of nowhere on the freeway, had something to do with it. So, what did my boss, in his infinite wisdom do? He hired a slightly older White woman who was tall, slim, and a cross between Linda Evans and Doris Day. The men in the office adored her. She and I hit it off really well. I saw her as an ally rather than competition. The other co-worker made negative comments about her. I listened, but I silently disagreed. She was friendly from what I could see.

It was not until it finally dawned on me that my boss had hired her to "oversee" the rest of us. Then I was really angry, not at her, at him. My skills were so great, yet I was always undercut from being able to move up in the company. The Linda-Doris employee said she had a degree but never had to produce it to prove it. Apparently, it had been so long ago, she'd have to have the schools dig through the archives to find it. OKAY. Then one day I actually overheard her and the other co-worker discussing me in not so friendly terms and plotting against me. I decided Linda-Doris was no longer my ally. To make matters worse, I confronted her about the remarks they had made. We had words. We both made biting remarks to each other, in front of the other staff. Not good. Not professional. Career suicide. I was placed back into the Word Processing Center. I was still a good worker. However, I was about to experience the wrath and political vengeance of the Linda-Doris person, who had now teamed up with the other Word Processing Specialist, who was more than willing to put the finishing touches on my dying career at Northrop.

Almost every day, I received phone calls at my phone extension from other staff where they screamed, burped, or farted on the other end. Usually, I just ignored it and hung up the phone. I couldn't believe how childish they were. Even though one of the other White females in the Word Processing Center had already been advised that she and two others would be transferred to the new start-up Word Processing Center about 10 miles away, my boss "decided" that I would be transferred over there instead. We lived within walking distance of the current facility. I could even walk home for lunch. That was about to come to an end. They put me over in a small room with no staff. Excuse me, it wasn't really a "room"; it was more like a "dungeon." They said because of my great skills and accomplishments, they knew I would make it a success. It was a small department with hardly any people there. On paper, they made it as though it was a lateral movement with great opportunity. However, they and I knew it was in reality, a demotion. I learned that even when you do well, if you don't play ball and kiss up to the right people, your career is still doomed. It's the same old adage: *"It's not what you know; it's who you know."* I didn't want this to be true, but there it was staring me in the face. I tried to make the best of it, but the gregarious people-person that I am conflicted with this solitary confinement. Each day, I hated going to work. The more I thought about it, the angrier I became.

I tried sending certified letters my boss's supervisor. However, this was something I'd never done before. I didn't know at the time that you had to actually take them to the post office yourself. All of our outgoing mail went through Northrop. Of course, at one our staff meetings, I overheard Linda-Doris and the other Word Processing Specialist giggling and laughing and making jokes about the problems with our "outgoing mail." I knew then that they had confiscated the mail. The other Word Processing Specialist told me that I had a "brain like nothing." I couldn't understand why they hated me so much. Then I remembered. As long as I stayed in my "place," as long as I laughed and joked and humiliated myself, as long as I portrayed the image of the good little "sapphire," they had no problem with me. It was only until I, like Kunta Kinte, determined that my name was not "Toby," they knew they would have to continue to whip me and whip me until I would eventually acquiesce.

Finally, someone told me I should file charges with the EEOC, the Equal Employment Opportunity Commission. Every employer who receives federal funds and who is required to submit and publicly display its anti-discrimination policy is supposed to be bound by this mandate. I have now come to learn that for me, this process is a joke and a waste of my valuable time. Unless you are willing to complete the process and actually take them to court and sue them, it is a wasted effort. David slew Goliath with only a sling and a rock. If you do not have the Rock, Jesus, on your side and it is not God's will, you're just flinging rocks into the air and wasting what little strength you have. If God is with you, he'll show you just where to hit the opponent – smack dab in the temple. He'll show you where the vulnerability lies. People always think becoming a Christian means they will have a bed of roses. This is because they come to Christ for the wrong reasons. What is that reason: because they've been told *"God has a wonderful plan for your life."* God does have a plan, but he expects repentance from the wrath to come. We are deserving of God's wrath because of our sin. Once we have repented and asked God for his forgiveness and turn from this, then and only then are we ready for His mercy. Only then can we experience and know the love of God that required Jesus' sacrifice on Calvary. Jesus paid the price for us. He paid our fine that would have required our death. We can now go free. But this freedom does not mean we will always get everything we want. We still suffer consequences for the things we've done in our lives. We still suffer because God is making us strong enough, molding us into what He wants us to be so we can be used by Him. Too bad I didn't understand all of this then. It would have saved me a lot of heartache. All I knew was that I had been treated unfairly by people who had benefited from all of the work I'd given them over the last five years. Five years – that was the longest I'd worked for any one company, other than my own. In fact, that was the last time I would give a company more than three years of my time, talent, and tears.

Well, there I was, sitting across from a Filipino woman at the EEOC. Of course, the department for whom I worked was in no way going to make the task easy. They first refused to cooperate, and then did everything in their power to intimidate me. My record was immaculate; I'd received commendations and a promotion, even a letter detailing my accomplishments. So, they couldn't say that I was not a good worker or a good employee. You see, the EEOC investigator told me she knew exactly what the company was doing. She knew exactly what they'd done to me, and that I had been wronged. There was just one little problem: she couldn't prove it. In order for her to proceed, she needed to have at least one other person within the department who had also been racially discriminated against. Well, I thought this was easy. There was one such person. I begged her to come forward. She told me they had threatened her. She said she didn't want to lose her job. She said her mother was dying of cancer. I understood her situation, but I knew it would not be long before they would do the same thing to her that they'd done to me. However, there was no way I would be able to convince her of this, so I left her alone.

Not sure how I heard about him, but someone recommended a doctor who dealt with matters of job-related stress. It seems he actually took them to court. I know I'd experienced a great deal of trauma behind what they did to me at the company. I was about to quit the company and sue them for "disability due to stress." One other employee at the company was experiencing what I'd gone through; of course, not the same person who I'd asked to help me. This was another Black woman. I told her about what I was going to do and she decided to do the same thing. Things didn't turn out the way either of us expected. I knew she was devastated and angry at me, but she had no idea what I went through. When we went to court to give our deposition, it was apparent that the company's attorney had unearthed the trauma that I'd experienced from my children being molested and taken from me. I don't swim very well, but if my children were drowning, I'd jump in to save them. If someone were firing a pistol at them, I'd jump in front of them to take the bullet. That day, in court, the company's attorney fired a huge torpedo at me. It totally caught me by surprise. He went through the scenario of my children's molestation and my being charged with neglect. He said this was due to my trauma and distress, not what I'd experienced at the company. I couldn't believe anyone would be so insensitive and of course, I told him so. We had words. My attorney wanted to pull me to the side and talk to me, but I answered all of the opposing attorney's questions anyway. Hard lesson learned: always listen to your attorney when the opposition is firing cannons at you. He'll show you how to deflect them.

I was granted a small sum, but a mere pittance compared to what I should have received. If only I'd closed my mouth. Where was wisdom when I needed her? The fear of God is the beginning of wisdom. Wisdom was on her way, but not until unemployment had had her say. My friend Keith bought a house. He moved my children and me into it. I bought the furniture and appliances. So, we played house for over two years. He taught me how to ski. He taught me how to ice skate. He taught me about computer hardware. He taught me how to go into a computer and change the "dip switch" to increase the memory. He helped me get my first computer. He gave me money every week. All I did was sleep with me and kept him company. I loved him then and I love him now. He was my best male friend. Anna was my best female friend. Michael was my other best male friend – just a friend.

I tried looking for another job. I thought surely the employers in Inglewood would be a little kinder. What luck, or so I thought, I found a company run by a young Black man. Surely he would understand my plight and recognize my skills and abilities. The White woman who greeted me told me that he was so wonderful, so great, and they all just love him. When I sat down with him I could the eyes of Satan. They say the eyes are the window to the soul. They are right. He casually glanced through my resume, and then looked down at me as if I were something gooey and disgusting stuck on the bottom of his shoe. He said, *"Good resume, but what have you done lately?"* And then came the wicked smile. What kind of employers quote, or rather misquote, Janet Jackson? I remembered the commercial that asked, *"Have you driven a Ford lately?"* This caused an Asian couple to retort, when asked what kind of car they wanted to buy, to say, "A Ford Lately." They'd heard the commercial so much but misunderstood it. They thought the name was "Ford Lately." This young Black crumb-scratcher dared to ask me what I'd done lately! I know that I had more skills and abilities in my little 30-year-old finger than he did in his whole envious body. I learned that Black people can be even more so discriminatory against their own race, especially Black men against Black women, while all the while these same men cater to White women. I just couldn't understand it.

Enough job hunting. Keith had bought me a computer. Time to put it to good use. With a computer in hand, I started my writing career and discovered the entrepreneurial spirit within me. I guess I'd always been a writer and an entrepreneur but never knew what that "restlessness" was. I never knew what that desire to innovate, to improve, to create, to design was. I started my own typing service. I did odd jobs for people. I never really made much money, but it was a start. I would love to say that this grew into a big company, but I can't, because it didn't. I didn't have the vision, the skills, or the funding for this at the time. However, I did love to write. I'd been writing little stories and poems since I was 18. I was almost 30 then. I wrote my first 300-page novel. It was based on a dream I'd had. I still remember that dream. It's funny: if I didn't know better, I would swear that the movie, Ghost, with Patrick Swayze, Whoopi Goldberg, and Demi Moore was based in part on my book. But I never sent it to anyone, so how could they get it? My main character's name was Sam but a female instead of male. Anyway, I remember Keith slobbering over the pages as he read them. It was the worst piece of filth and trash that I'd ever written and was ever going to write. When I think back, I'm not sure how I could have written such trash. It would have been a best seller. I'd have made my million I'd always wanted to make, and I'd have been "successful." But "what does a man profit if he gains the whole world yet lose his own soul?" I would soon find out.

God wasn't through pulling on his fishing line. I wasn't sure if Keith was really an atheist of if he was more of an agnostic like I used to call myself. He never really espoused to any religious belief, nor did he ever attend church, that I knew of. I was taking a few classes at El Camino Community College. I was on a quest to work on getting my degree. I took Economics, Theatre, and Writing. I enjoyed the classes. I encountered students who were always in religious debates on campus. This was my first experience with people who did "open air preaching." Gangs of White students would gather around the preacher and yell insults and try to debate issues with him. I found myself engrossed in one conversation where the aggressor told the preacher that he'd previously been to seminary and knew the ins and outs of the Bible. I heard one of his buddies yell, *"Go ahead K, give it to him. Tell him what you know."* I didn't know the Bible that well, but I had started reading and studying it. I had also started going to church. I mentioned Romans, Chapter 1, versus 18 through 24 that talks about the sin of homosexuality. It was so odd, the look he had on his face. I now know the look was one of conviction. Strange. The power of God's word. He grew very silent. I didn't say it to him to judge him. I said it as more of a question to him. The crowd couldn't understand why he was silent. I realized even at that time that he was gay and that he'd left seminary because of it. It would be years before I would realize and accept that I was not paranoid. I came to understand that God had given me a gift to foresee things and to see things about people's lives. Too bad it took me a long time to see these things about my own life.

That year, my spiritual search would take me to workshops with people who chanted and worshipped crystals. It took me in front of Christian Scientists who chain smoked and told me they could rid me of *my* obvious aberrations. It took me on a weekend mountain retreat with people who were fun, young, and talented, and who told me that Reverend Moon was Christ who'd come back. They assured me that it was my "job" to give up my children and come serve the Reverend Moon. That was one job I definitely didn't want. My search took me through different churches. No matter what, I still read my Bible, or tried to do so. I thought I was a smart, learned individual. I was a reader. I felt if you wanted to learn anything, just read about it. I started reading the Bible at the beginning. My goal was to go all the way to the end, and of course, then I would know all I should know. Right? Wrong. Every time I would get to the part in Genesis where God asked Abraham to offer his son up for a sacrifice, I couldn't read anymore. I was so angry. How could God do that? It was all nonsense.

I told my friend Michael about this and he told me I was starting in the wrong place. What did he mean, "Starting in the wrong place?" I told him I was starting at the beginning. He said, "Just start in the New Testament." I did just that. I now know why. The New Testament tells of him. By the time I got back to Genesis, I could go forward. I finally saw that God had a "ram in the bush," like he always does. God said he would "provide himself a sacrifice." This is just what he did when Jesus died on Calvary. It all made sense. I knew why Michael had me start at Matthew in the New Testament. Before you can get to God, you first have to come to Christ. I had always been afraid of death. The devil made me feel that if I totally committed to God, I was going to die. He was right. However, the "death" was death to self, the old life, and my sins. I won't go into more detail because this book is more about work and employment than it is about my spiritual conversion. What I can say is after Christ interceded for me and I experienced the deep hole of nothingness within the pit of my soul, and I experienced what it was like to really die for a short period of time, God called me to the ministry. I am now and have been from that day forward employed by God – employed in every sense of the word. He is and will always be my boss and my overseer. It's not easy working for God, but the retirement benefits are eternal.

I was employed as an Ambassador for Christ. Get ready for a life of rejection. Get ready for a life of trials and not so happy trails. Get ready for a life of mercy and grace and love. Whatever I went through, my employer was right there taking me through it. I was and am never alone. After my experience with God and my call to the ministry, my employer was relocating me to another place. When I found myself prostrate before God, my face down, and hands arms spread out in resignation to His will, I asked Him what he wanted me to do. He said, among other things, He wanted me to come back home. Now you must realize that when God tells you something, it's not usually in audible words, He speaks to your spirit and then He confirms what He says in His word and in other ways. His words also have more depth, breadth and width than people realize. Yes, he wanted me to come back home to Him, and yes, he wanted me to come back home to where I was born. The place where he'd originally planted His seed in my heart. My employer was relocating me back to Arizona, the desert, the wilderness, the dry and barren place. I was going to be tried in the fire. My friend Linda, with whom I grew up, would forever liken my experience in Arizona as "rowing upstream with only one oar." She was right.

When God says go, you don't question His will. I felt like Abraham, being called out of my country, out of my comfort zone, out into unknown territory. My faith was so strong; I would follow God to the ends of the earth if he asked me to do so. With Keith's help and God's providence, I left all of my furniture, but I had $600 and my car when we ended up in Phoenix, Arizona. Keith drove us there in my Buick. When he got on the plane to leave, I sat there on the corner of 7th Avenue and Dunlap for a few minutes with little ones in the back seat and just stared ahead. Now what, Lord, I thought to myself. Well, I was going to need a place to stay, childcare, and a job. Why? Because my children would need to eat, and eventually, so would I. I first tried signing up with DES (Dept. of Economic Security) so I could have something coming in while searching for employment. The Black man in the office looked at me like I was scum and a freeloader. I could tell I would not be getting anything soon or very easily. Not being familiar with the area or how much things cost, I rented a motel room for us. It cost $100 a week. The carpet was filthy, the stove didn't work, the mattresses were torn, and it was roach infested. I remembered coming home one day and I happened to see the landlady coming out of the motel room next to ours. She had just finished vacuuming. It was immaculate. I was devastated. How could she do that do me, knowing that I had little children? We stayed there two weeks. I found a room to rent from a woman who turned out to be crazy. She had a deranged daughter, a deranged boyfriend, and a deranged cat.

I applied for several jobs. I couldn't believe the low pay they were offering. I'd made $12 an hour at Northrop. I remember applying for a simple file clerk position. I was obviously over-qualified for it. The manager, who hadn't seen my resume, told me it was more than just a file clerk position. I told him that was fine because I was more than just a file clerk. I gave him my resume. After looking it over, he asked me if I knew some ridiculous thing that had absolutely nothing to do with the position. Of course I told him I didn't. He said I had to have that in order to do the job. Good day. I finally signed up with a temporary agency that placed me at the Maricopa Skills Center. It was familiar. It reminded me of the Watts Skills Center. Only this time my days of thievery were behind me. I worked there for two weeks before my car engine froze on me. I had so much to do that it never dawned on me to check my oil. A call to my friend Keith and he sent me money to get a new engine, which did not cost much for an old car like that. In the meantime, I had to leave the house of the deranged woman. I'd put up with everything they'd done from putting us in a room with no door where we were visited constantly by the deranged cat, and putting ice cubes in the refrigerator shaped like phallic symbols just to see how I would react. I ignored it all. My children would sit in the living room with them and watch TV. I stayed in my room when I came home from work after picking them up from the babysitter.

I hadn't really thought of contacting my uncle until then. We moved in with him and a friend with whom he was staying. I liked her; she was a school counselor. My assignment at the Maricopa Skills Center was up. The temporary agency sent me on an assignment where I had to stuff envelopes for $4 an hour. Apparently the young White girl they'd sent told them that she wasn't hired to stuff envelopes. She said she was hired to type. I told them, *"I'll stuff envelopes."* There is dignity in all work, and I knew my babies had to eat. I worked with several young people who knew I was a Christian but they insisted on cracking filthy jokes. One of them appeared to be "just out of the closet," and made a point to make sure everyone knew it. I remembered how horrid I must have been to the two men at Northrop who had given me the look that convicted me. I gave these young people the same look. Funny, it didn't have the same effect on them. I was so glad when the assignment ended.

The temporary agency sent me out on another assignment that was extremely far away. I had to use the money Keith sent to make ends meet. I really don't remember whatever happened to that car. As once before in my life, the bus was my new best friend. The bus system in Arizona was not as progressive as that in

California. The scheduled runs were at least 30 minutes to an hour in between. It took me three buses to get to where the assignment was. I arrived there early and on time. It was a two-man insurance office. They needed a receptionist. I always dressed nice and presentable, but there was no way I could change my skin color or the texture and/or color of my hair. It seems I would always be a Black woman. I really liked this about myself, but a great number of people seemed to have a serious problem with it. I remembered being on the bus one day. I felt an overwhelming feeling of rejection. At that moment, I was going to ask a Hispanic man about the racism in Arizona. I didn't get a chance to finish my sentence. I said, *"Does it seem . . .?"* He said, *"Exactly what you're feeling is exactly what it is."* God has angels everywhere. They work for Him too. Their jobs are many, mostly to praise Him and watch over his people. I've encountered many of them in human form.

When I arrived at the assignment, the man was pleasant but surprised to see me. And then a White girl, a young gum-chewer, showed up, who told me she was just doing this until she could go to Hollywood to do modeling and then become an actress. She was thin and blonde, but I didn't have the heart to tell her that she'd have to almost sell her body and her soul to make it in that business in Hollywood. After she arrived, the two men discovered that they both had called a temporary agency. I realized then and there that their business would probably not prosper if they didn't communicate with each other enough to know what the other was doing. They told us they would have to go in the back and discuss how they would handle the situation. Even though we discovered that my agency had been contacted the day before Miss Hollywood's temporary agency, I told them to let her have the position. I told them no discussion would be needed. I knew that after a day or so of her, they'd realize they should have used me, but I decided I'd let them find that out on their own. Also, it was my experience that what they really were going to do was make up what they considered to be a viable excuse as to why they were going to use her instead of me. I had no doubt that God was going to bless me.

I knew I'd traveled a long way to get to the assignment and I felt a bit of unfairness, but there was no bitterness. I'd come through so much and it made me stronger. There was a woman on the bus stop next to me. She confided in me about a few things and I confided in her about my recent experience and how I let the other girl take the assignment. The woman was impressed with my good deed. On the way home I thought about how much I'd changed. When I got home, my uncle told me I had a message from the temporary agency. They'd heard about what happened. They commended me on what I'd done. They told me that because I had been so faithful, they had a long-term assignment for me that paid $8 an hour at Phelps Dodge Corporation. I was excited and grateful.

It would only take two weeks before my supervisor offered me a full-time position with the company. It would pay $10 an hour and I would have benefits. He was willing to pay the temporary agency the early release fee required. Boy, I thought, I must be good. I remember my uncle commenting how I could get jobs at companies that most people couldn't. It was true, but it was God's hand on me. He was my employer and He opened up the doors, but He also closed them when it was time. I was a strange person, but such are God's prophets. We don't always do and say what people think we should, and we are human like everyone else, despite our spiritual gifts. I worked with a thin Asian girl. The Executive Assistant who worked upstairs with the big boss was Hawaiian and had hair down to her ankles. She was thin, attractive and professional in her demeanor. My supervisor was a middle-aged White man who seemed overly protective of the office. He didn't want me to work overtime or even stay a few minutes past 5:00 PM. I kept thinking he was hiding something or maybe he felt I would learn more than just my job and learn his. Either way, he was odder than I was.

I did learn a lot there. In fact, I learned more about copper mining than I cared to know. In actuality, I thought what they did was completely boring. However, what they did was completely lucrative. I tired of shaving my legs and the hair that was growing on my face. I believe some of the women in our family were cursed with hair. Too much of it grew in the wrong places. I was over 30, in love with God, didn't need a man, and didn't see the need for expensive and bothersome, burning hair remover. So, I opted out of it. Some of the staff would stare at me. It actually humored me. I knew I was being defiant and I didn't care. I was so tired of society's superficial focus on the way people looked. Everything was image. I saw so much deception. Great people rejected because they didn't look a certain way. Despicable people praised and promoted because they were good looking. I was never mean to anyone. I was always loving and gracious, but I had hair on my legs and face. I did stand up and speak out against injustices I saw. I defended people at the company who later left me high and dry because they were afraid of losing their jobs. I had no goals for advancement and didn't care what people thought. I worked there for six months and decided it was time to leave. I quit and went back to another temporary agency.

Temporary agencies were my mainstay in between "permanent" jobs. By this time, my uncle was buying some apartments in Glendale. We first stayed with him and then rented one of the apartments from him. I remember taking some of his towels and other things with us because there were quite a few things we didn't have. I figured he wouldn't mind, but now that I think about it, I should have asked him first. My uncle never took me seriously when it came to my spiritual calling. In fact, he laughed when I shared one of my experiences with him. His impression has always been that I had book knowledge but not very much common sense. Of course, he had a great deal of common sense. Not sure about his book knowledge. He was very good at B.S. so it didn't matter if he had the degree or not. He acted like he did.

The temporary agency found a short-term position for me with a company on Greenway Avenue. It was further north than where I lived. I liked it because I was working with computers. I figured out a faster way of doing things on the system. The office manager was nice but it appeared she hadn't worked there very long and she was trying her best not to step on anyone's toes. My supervisor was another story. She had a bad back, wore 2-inch heels, was mean as all get out, and didn't care on whose toes she stepped. I could tell she didn't like me very much. I hadn't done anything to her except know my job really, really well. It wasn't until later that I finally realized that a spirit would continue to follow me all of the days of my life, especially in the field of work. This spirit came from the pit of Hell and was called envy, resentment, and insecurity. People with whom I worked would forever feel threatened by me. I thought if I was only a temporary employee, this wouldn't be the case, but it happened nonetheless.

Although it's not as sharp as it used to be, I have a semi-photographic memory. I usually remember what I see and especially what I type. I was a fast typist when it came to keying in data. The supervisor called me in one day and showed me pages of information that she said I typed and all the errors that she had circled. I looked over the pages and immediately knew that I had not typed them. She told me that I needed to slow down and be more careful in what I'm doing. She said that if I didn't, they would have to let me go. I said nothing. She asked me if I had any questions, I shook my head "no." I remember that instead of catching the bus to work, I rode my bike all the way from Glendale Avenue to Greenway. It was a long way, but I got there on time and was proud of myself. I told them I'd ridden my bike. My supervisor seemed displeased. I think part of it was because she had a bad back and couldn't ride a bike. I wonder if she ever realized that her 2-inch heels didn't help the situation. I would never find out because the next day when I came in, the office manager told me that they were letting me go. My supervisor was such a coward. She couldn't face me herself. Before I left, I put yellow "Stickles" on everyone's desk with Scripture on them. I prayed that God's words would convict them all. The office manager couldn't believe I was doing that. She hung her head. I knew then that she felt I was being let go unjustly.

Undaunted, I was back on the job search circuit. I landed a part-time job at the YMCA in Metro Center. I liked it. I had my own small office and I sent notices to individuals requesting that they honor their donation pledges to the "Y." It seemed like a dream job. However, my nightmare was just about to show up. My ex-husband contacted me, spoke to the kids, and told us how well he was doing at Victory Outreach. He was working and preaching there. However, he missed us all and wanted to come to Arizona to live with us. It didn't dawn on me at the time that it things were that great, why would he want to leave? I was now a different person and asked God what to do. I couldn't understand at the time why I had to get back together with my husband, but I did as God led me. I was close to God. I thought he was too. Just maybe things would work. Yes, I am the eternal optimist. I sent him a plane ticket to come to Arizona. He found odd jobs and very rarely worked. It was the same scenario all over again. But before this, he was at home keeping the kids, so I trusted him with my bank account in case they needed money. It wasn't until a friend of mine told me she saw my car parked down on 24th Street & Van Buren that I realized my mistake. She gave me a ride down there after work. My ex-husband was stoned out of his mind. My bank account was empty and he said the car was "broke." The car wasn't broken. He'd run out of gas and was too loaded to realize it. We got both the car and him back home.

I was so miserable during that time. He was taking my money and buying drugs with it. I tried to focus on his good points. He did go to church intermittently. He had praised me and appeared to support me when I had my first article published. I had interviewed the couple when I was in California. It wasn't until I had moved to Arizona that I received the check from the magazine. Even though he praised me, I could tell there was still envy there. He had always wanted to attend USC; I went to USC. He had always wanted to write. I had not only written something, but had it published. I am a firm believer that a woman, especially a Black woman should never marry someone who is not her equal in education. If he is a man of God and God has put her with the man, then that is God's will. In this case, it can work.

I remember my ex-husband would leave church early to go have a drink. He told me about seeing one of the choir members as he was passing by the XXX adult movie stores on his way home. He kept laughing saying that the choir member had just gotten his tapes all settled, fastened his seat belt, and then looked up to see my ex-husband staring at him. The choir member's head went down in embarrassment. Of course, I never mentioned to the choir member that I knew. We all have done wrong and I guess he was no different. That was something he had to work out with God. Just like my ex-husband and me. My ex-husband was getting on my nerves. He was so jealous of other men, especially White men. I remembered one day being in the park and he was harassing me. I yelled out to God, *"I don't want to be married!"* We should be careful what we say. What I meant was I didn't want to be married to my ex-husband, but that's not what I said. Maybe that's one of the reasons that after 26 years of divorce, I'm still single.

I was working everyday but I was still broke. My ex-husband was taking my money. I paid my rent on time and I paid my tithes faithfully. I went to my pastor and told him what my ex-husband was doing. He would always say, *"Ah, Sister, we have to pray for Brother K."* Things got so bad my ex-husband started taking my tithe money he'd hunted down which was inside my Bible. When I told this to my pastor, he said, *"Oh no, K has to go."* I guess it was fine when Brother K was taking my money, but when he started taking the church's share, he had to go. In addition, it was getting to where I couldn't pay my rent. My pastor had a talk with my landlord. The decision was that the children and I could stay, but ex-husband had to go. He didn't take this too well and left the state. He went back to California. I tried to get him to stay, but he was selfish. Because he could no longer live with us, he was not going to try to do right and live and work for us.

I thank God for temporary employment agencies. They were always my mainstay in between full-time jobs. I was placed on an assignment at The Dial Corporation in downtown Phoenix. I had two supervisors, both slender White women, for a change. I adored them. DR had a wonderful sense of humor and was the Director of Employee Benefits. LH was a bit more businesslike and was the Director of Compensation. They both reported to Mr. B, the Vice President of Human Resources. I enjoyed my job and learned a lot, as usual. I was hired on a permanent basis. It was the same thing again. The first year was Heaven and the second year a living Hell.

I was hired as an administrative assistant (secretary to the layperson). My station was out in the open, so I was also receptionist. My area was enclosed by a professional booth-like counter that afforded me a great deal of room. My area was next to the Vice President's administrative assistant. One of the attorneys on whom I had a crush at the time compared the two of us. He referred to her as a Volkswagen and to me as a Cadillac; however, he said that she, in her limited capacity, functioned to the best of her ability. He said this because I had started taking tuition-reimbursed classes at the University of Phoenix and had received a "C" in my Business Law class and told him I thought the grade was doing "OK." He said he was a Christian also and had high ideals that I would learn later that he did more talking about than he what he actually lived.

Office politics are not and have never been my forte. However, trouble always seemed to find me. I always try to mind my own business and not bother anyone. I stay away from gossip as much as possible. Why is it that I am always the person to whom facts come? As time would go on, I would learn very slowly how to deal with these situations, but The Dial Corporation was another experience teacher. Since I worked in Personnel, I was privy to employment information for the company. I knew when positions became available. I saw resumes. I took phone calls for my supervisors and for the Vice President when his secretary was away. The Director of Communications position became available. However, it had not been posted and I was getting returned calls from specific individuals whom the Vice President had contacted about the position. I read the job description. I was a writer and I knew I could do the job. I didn't have the savvy, the connections, a world-traveler background, or the prior employment background beyond a supervisor of a Word Processing Department. However, I knew that, given the opportunity, I could do the job. When it came to the field of work and office politics, little did I know that I would have a lot more to learn.

I applied for the position. A week later I was called into a meeting with both of my supervisors. You would have thought I had committed a crime. It was worse: I had dared to apply for a position on the same level as them. They questioned me as to why I applied for the position. I told them simply that I believed I could do the job. They proceeded to tell me that you needed a degree for the position. I realized I had put them all in an awkward position by applying for the position before it was posted. The policy was that the position should be posted internally first to give all qualified employees an opportunity to seek the position before seeking a viable applicant outside of the company. They had obviously violated policy. It became apparent to me that I had a choice of pursuing the situation or pulling out. I also realized from the meeting and my supervisors' demeanors that I would not receive an interview nor would I have a chance in receiving the position. I opted to pull out.

They hired a crude and rude person who got along very well with the attorney with whom I had been previously enamored and likened me to a cadillac. One of my supervisors got along with her while the other one told me, "She doesn't make me feel very good about myself, so I try not to deal with her very much." The Director of Communications was, I must say, a good writer and very effective. I learned that you can jump through a million hoops and still never satisfy the "powers that be."

I can't say that my two years there was not all bad. The attorney and LH gave me tickets to some of the sporting events and a musical. They were tickets, of course, that they were not going to use, and they were free. I was grateful, nonetheless. Almost every week on every floor of that building there was a party, I mean, business meeting. I have never seen so much food in my life just go to waste. I truly believe they could have fed the entire third world countries with the amount of food they threw away every week. A few times I took what I could home to my kids.

One of my supervisors, DR, always presented herself as a Christian woman. I liked her sense of humor and her down-to-earth personality. Most executives wanted you to throw away the junk mail like magazines, ads, and direct mail. Not DR. She told me, *"I like the junk mail."* So, I saved it all for her to look through every day. I remember she invited me over to her house for the Christmas holiday to spend the night with her husband and her children. By that time, for some unexplained reason, I lost one of my contacts and had to wear my thick bifocals. The attorney and a few other co-workers also spent Christmas over at DR's house. I spent most of the time to myself working my crossword puzzle. I had put my kids on a plane to California to spend Christmas with my parents. I guess DR felt sorry for me. We even went to church the next day. I thoroughly enjoyed myself.

There is a scripture that says, "Weeping may endure for a night, but joy comes in the morning." When it comes to the work world, it should be changed to, "Joy may endure for a night, but weeping comes in the morning." There were times when I wished I had not believed in being "my brother's keeper." In this case, it was my "sister's keeper." There were whispers and gossip around the office, but for the life of me I had no idea who or what they were talking about, nor did I care. I soon found out what was going on. So, I asked God, *"Why me?"* He said, *"Just a minute,"* and it was almost a decade before I got my answer.

DR had called in sick for two days. I was her secretary, so I just took care of everything, took messages, and did what she asked me to do. Not a problem. I remember the Vice President asking me if DR was coming in that day. I told him I thought so, since I hadn't heard from her. I saw him go into her office, but I didn't really pay much attention to it. After all, he was her supervisor. About an hour later, she called me. She said she would be in later and she wanted me to go into her office to look for something. I put her on hold and went into her office. Of course I had the key. I picked up the phone in her office and started searching for what she had asked. Just as she said, *"Do you see it?"* I saw a note that the Vice President had left for her. It said, *"Darling, I miss you. I enjoyed our night and our kiss. Love ..."* I was dumbfounded. I could hardly speak. I managed to say, *"Y-Yes ... I found it."*

There are many opportunists out there who would have thought to either blackmail the people involved since they were both married. Some would have even considered suing the company for being subjected to such emotional turmoil. Unfortunately for me, I am like none of those people. If only I had not spent a weekend with her wonderful Christian family. If only I had not been concerned and cared. I know the best thing would have been to just keep my mouth shut and never say anything to DR, but like I said, wisdom was coming very slowly back then. DR listened intently while I told her about my concerns for her. I wanted to make sure she wasn't the victim of sexual harassment. She assured me she was all right, and told me a little about how the involvement with the Vice President occurred. I, like the fool I was, believed her.

It was a few day after this that I saw the powers that be, including the Vice President, my two supervisors, and the attorney having meetings. The attorney even approached me to feel me out and see whether or not I was planning anything. I guess they never really believed that anybody like me could exist, that I wouldn't one day try to use the information I had. I tried to forget about the event after it happened. DR left the company and left her husband. The Vice President left his wife and he and

DR got married. I guess they lived happily ever after, but I didn't. In fact, the attorney was very hard on me. He said, "Don't you know you're not White! You can't go around being friends with these people. They don't care a thing about you." This attorney was good looking on the outside, but he was so ugly and hypocritical on the inside. He slept around and cussed, but he told me he went to church every week. I started to tell him that going to church was not going to save him, but I decided he would just argue the point. However, when it came to assessing the situation, he was definitely right.

I really cannot explain it, but it seems as though White people, who are not truly saved people of God, can be so vicious and vengeful. You would think this applies to anyone who is not a saved woman or man of God, but from my experiences, White people are so calculating. Most Black people will let you know up front where you stand with them. If they don't like you and are against you, you usually know it. White people will smile in your face and stab you in the back at the same time. Mind you, I'm speaking solely from my own experience. I do realize that evil knows no color.

We all worked in Personnel, so I always thought of us as one. Wrong again. One of the managers who reported to my supervisor seemed to befriend me and I her. I remember she opened up to me one day in her office about a few things in her life. I tried to empathize with her but could only sympathize with the things she said. She had a great job, made a lot more money than I did, had a husband, and a nice office. She had one of the other co-workers and me to act as her "gophers." Still, I felt that I would try to cheer her up when the opportunity presented itself. The opportunity came and took my job security with it. Since I worked for LH who was the Director of Compensation, I was always privy to everyone's salary, including pay increases and bonuses. Funny, how this trend of being the lowest paid person in the company with knowledge of everyone's salary would follow me for a long time to come. I never divulged salaries or pay increases to anyone. However, the manager, along with several others in the company, was going to receive an extra bonus and recognition. I confided in the manager about this because I thought I was helping her. I did add that she might think about sharing a minute percentage of her bonus with the other co-worker who I knew worked her buns off. She asked me if there were others who were receiving bonuses and I told her that a few others were. I thought it was safe to share it with her because I thought of her as another supervisor, and like I said, we all worked in the same department.

To make a long story short, my supervisor called me in. The manager had not gone to my supervisor. She had gone to the Vice President with the info. I was temporarily suspended and sent home. In the meantime, they had hired a Black woman to replace DR. She also had a legal background in addition to Employee Benefits. I waited one day, then went back to the office and demanded that they tell me whether or not I was fired right then and there. I told them I had no intention of allowing them to draw the whole thing out. The decision was that the information would go into my file. This meant that I would not ever be eligible for any type of promotion and possibly no future pay increases. The Black woman said we would chalk this up to experience and move forward. She had no idea and knowledge of what was really going on. It didn't take me long to figure out that the manager who reported me had been trying to get me fired and that she was retaliating. However, I still couldn't figure out what I had done to her that was so wrong. So I asked her. It's funny; I've learned that if you listen to people long enough, eventually they will tell you the real motives behind their actions. At first, she insisted that she felt I was breaching confidentiality. She said I had spoiled the surprise for her. Then it came. She said, *"Plus, I didn't appreciate you telling me what to do with my own money."* There it was. Her own guilty conscience had convicted her. She groaned and complained about her life, but I had shown her how good she had it compared to others who were not as well off as she was. I had merely suggested that she share her wealth. She had been insulted by it. I believe capitalism sucks, but so does communism and socialism. People are so selfish and want to have more than others to make themselves feel special. They really don't care if other people are homeless and are eating dirt, as long as they, themselves, have everything they could ever want. Unfortunately, the manger was one of those people. She also knew about the incident that led to DR leaving the company and marrying the Vice President. There it was. They had waited and baited until they could get something on me. In their minds, this would prevent me from ever trying to use the information I had. They never knew and realized that even if they had fired me, I would never have tried to do anything to them.

When management is okay with you, people in the office surround you. They laugh at your jokes. They enjoy your poems (I wrote several on different occasions) and they share information with you. When something like the foregoing incident occurs, people treat you like you have the plague. It's as if they believe you'll be fired any minute and they don't want to be affected or infected by it. I had some dark spots in my Christian walk during that time. When I started to truly let my light shine, the persecutions came. If the world loves you, especially the work world, you had better check your light bulb, as Tyler Perry's *Madea* character would say.

Whenever God closes a door, believe me, he always opens up another one. This has always been my experience. I had joined a group called Toastmasters. Instead of giving a speech, I recited a poem. One of the members, Karen, took an interest in helping me. She happened to be an engineer at Motorola. I soon learned that knowing someone was an excellent way to get your foot in the door into a company like Motorola. Karen knew of a position that was open. She told the managers in Human Resource about me. I was so grateful for the opportunity to interview. I got the job. The attorney kept kidding me about having to go to Motorola to "pee in a cup" because they did background checks and drug testing. This was a requirement for employment and supposedly, you were subjected to have random drug testing.

I was so happy to be able to give my two-week notice at The Dial Corporation. The attorney had always insinuated that he and I would have a chance if we weren't working together, since he didn't date people with whom he worked. The day I was leaving he announced that he was getting married. To this day, I have kept that same philosophy. I never date men with whom I worked. Of course, this is easy when you're a black woman in Arizona, since the viable prospects are slim and you're not the wanted commodity. As a matter of fact, it's easy when you're a black woman anywhere, not just Arizona. But I digress....

Motorola, Inc. was the next corporation of my list of employment experiences. Funny, how we're always expectant the day we're hired, even exuberant. Nothing good ever lasts and things never stay the same, whether good or not so good. This, in and of itself, can be one's peace in the storm of uncertainty. Motorola was actually the first company to hire me outright without having to go through a temporary agency and prove my abilities first. Why? One of their female engineers knew me and what I was going through at The Dial Corporation. She knew of a position opening up in Personnel, put in a good word for me, and I got the interview. I had two direct supervisors again: both white women; one thin, the other not as thin. The thin one's name reminded me of a song; the other one's name reminded me of a man's name. However, in reality, I had 5 supervisors.

As usual, when you're just starting out anywhere, everyone was friendly and nice to you, at least externally. I had been blessed with somewhat of a photographic memory, so I decided to impress them the first day. If I remember correctly, there was a staff of eight altogether. They had "stand-up" meetings every morning. They did this to keep open communication among the staff and bring everyone up to speed on what had occurred the previous day. It only lasted maybe 5-10 minutes. The first day after I'd been introduced to everyone, I told them to cover their badges. I told them I had remembered their names. Two of three of them switched places to see if they could fool me. I correctly named them all. They were impressed and warmed up to me. I knew I'd made a good first impression. Little did I know the enemy was lurking in the wings, as usual.

I was competent and gung-ho. Everything I did, I did to the best of my ability and thoroughly and completely. My father taught me this. He instilled in me to perfect whatever I do. I remember as a child coming home with all A's and a B. My father wanted to know why I'd gotten a B. The people at Motorola in the Personnel Dept. had no clue that I was a Type A personality, that I strove for perfection, that at that time I strove toward accomplishments because of the lack I felt inside, because of the detrimental harm previous co-workers had imposed upon me. Some people are driven to go on shooting sprees and blow up buildings. I was driven to proving myself. I felt that just maybe if I can show them how good I am, they would for once overlook the dark brown skin that represented hundred years of slavery that represented ignorance in the minds of ignorant people that represented a forgotten people who never have and never will receive reparations for the wrong that has been done to them. As I write this, there is a black male president in the White House. However, contrary to popular belief, he's not the first black president. Our country had several black presidents before George Washington. However, America, as the United States has had four black presidents. However, Barrack Obama is the first whose pigmentation makes it evident and the first to acknowledge his half-African roots. Today, Obama espouses everyone getting a bachelor's degree and the importance of such. As I write this, in Arizona there are close to 800,000 people not enrolled in high school who are without a high school diploma, GED, or equivalent. During my days at Motorola, I did not feel a college degree proved one's intelligence. I knew more and could write better than those I'd seen with degrees. I felt it was "just a piece of paper."

The people with whom I worked, who had that piece of paper, resented and were envious of my accomplishments. I got to write small articles for the in-house newsletter. I assisted with new employee orientation. I became the Travel Reduction Coordinator and met with individuals at the City of Phoenix to help design campaigns to get others to carpool or use the vanpool. I became the File Retention Coordinator. I got our department involved in the Needy Family Program during Christmastime. It would take a while before I would learn that good leaders don't do everything themselves, even though most of them can. Good leaders allow others to participate and even ask for ideas from others. The problem was I didn't see myself as a leader back then.

My salary had improved and so did my housing. I received a referral from the people at Motorola to lease an apartment in Scottsdale where Motorola was located. Before this, I was living way across town in West Phoenix. It was a long and hot drive since it was summertime. I know they only rented to me because I worked at Motorola, had been referred by them, and made a decent salary. I had learned very early in life that a minority in America, especially a black woman with children, was not somebody people actually cared about. Yes, they received grant monies for social programs for providing needed services to us, but when it came to really helping you become self-sufficient or getting help from entities that were not social programs, we were and are on our own.

There are some things that if you tell them to people, they'd never believe you. What I'm about to recount is so bizarre that had I not lived through it, I too would not believe it. He was dark and handsome. Yes, he was a black man and good looking. He would later become part of a dark poem I wrote. He was living with a woman who he later married and divorced. He was mysterious, had an enticing smile, seemed harmless, and I broke my own rule: I became involved with a man with whom I worked. It took me a long time to figure out why sexual sins are so powerful and the easiest to which you can fall prey. I realized that sex is so powerful that it creates life – life that God gave to us. The Devil uses this medium and has used it down through the ages to destroy kingdoms and nations, case in point, Sodom and Gomorrah. When you are out of God's will, when you are not in prayer and reading the Bible, that is, not in direct communion with God, the enemy will find where you live and move in. He is so subtle and cunning and he stings you so quickly that you don't realize you've been poisoned until you're close to death, spiritual death.

The group of us came together through an organization of engineers. Not all of us, including me, were engineers, but we are associated with each other. He definitely was not an engineer. He was a witch. He told me he was a white witch, something I'd never heard of. In my book, a witch is a witch. I found this out after I'd already fallen for him. I experienced him do things to other people and to me. I heard him tell me about how he knew he had this type of power. He told me about a death for which he was responsible for "knowing about." However, I had three people around me die. Because of the nature of what happened and the circumstances of what he said and did, I knew he was responsible. However, he and I both knew I couldn't prove it. I never said anything to him or anyone else. My friend tried to warn me about him when he used to try to hit on me. Her son was shot and killed the day after the witch showed up at my house with a gun. When I asked him why he bought a gun, he said he had a stereo, a car, and other things, but he didn't have a gun. I thought it was strange, but didn't ask him anything further. He had been an acquaintance of my friend's son. Funny, he was the one that led the collection of money for her son. He didn't want to ride with us to take the money to her. He said he would come later. It was strange how he arrived about a half hour before us. He was holding her granddaughter in his lap when we got there. I tried to roundabout ask her questions regarding his acquaintance with her son, but it went nowhere. Six months later, her mother died. Six months after this, after I'd left Motorola, my friend died.

I remember David's sin with Bathsheba. They had a child and it was stillborn. David had lied, murdered, and committed adultery. As a result, he had war in his household. His own son rose up against him in rebellion. One of his sons raped his sister. One of his sons killed the other. When sin exists, there is shedding of blood. The Hebrews killed a lamb or small animal for the remission of their sins. They offered this upon the altar. Christ was the last lamb and his blood was shed for all of humanity. Because of his sacrifice, we no longer are under the penalty of the law. Yet out of my sin was a pregnancy. I allowed my sin to be covered by the shedding of this child's blood. I had an abortion. I had three abortions previous to this in my lifetime. Two of which were my ex-husbands. I was foolish, ignorant, ambitious, prideful, confused, and lost during those times. I had promised myself I would never have another one. Since he was living with another woman, he was determined that I would have an abortion. He even threatened to run me over if I didn't comply. He paid for everything. I went to his doctor and he went with me. I guess this was to make sure it was done.

Having an abortion is murder. It doesn't matter how people try to smooth it over. It doesn't matter the reasons or the circumstances. The child is God's blessing.

It was the act I was involved in that was sinful. We talk about Pro Choice. However, the child is never given a choice. The child is never given a chance to say, "*I want to live.*" *I want to become someone great one day. Mom, trust God. It will be all right. You'll see.*" Though I didn't directly murder the child, by having an abortion, this made me an accessory. Either way, God holds us accountable for every decision we make. Having an abortion is the worst wear and tear a woman could have on her womb. A doctor told me years later that I was lucky that my uterine lining didn't tear, causing me to bleed to death. He said having an abortion is like barreling down the freeway at 90 miles per hour and then suddenly throwing your car into reverse. The damage this does to your car is nothing compared to the damage this does to a woman's body. And last but not least, when a woman is pregnant, she goes through nine months carrying a child, dealing with morning or evening sickness, stretch marks, being overweight, swollen feet, out of control hormones, and countless other symptoms. She even has to bear through labor pains for the child to be born. But when this is all over, she usually will have a beautiful and healthy child to hold in her arms. In cases where the child is stillborn, there was usually sin prior to this, sometimes on the part of the mother; sometimes on the part of the father – sad to say, but true.

However, an abortion is an altogether different matter. You have no beautiful child to hold in your arms. You've gone through excruciating pain with nothing to show for it. All your labor has been in vain. He made sure my physical pain was cut short. As I lie there afterwards, he touched me. Immediately, the pain went away and I found myself almost giddy. He smiled that devilish smile. I was grateful for the relief, but greatly disturbed by his powers.

Had I remained a good little girl and not tried to share what I feared about him, I may have still had my job at Motorola. I sat in the courtyard during lunch one day with another male co-worker. I remember there was mist in the back. They did this to make sure it stayed cool out there. I know for a fact that he was not there. As I began to talk to the co-worker and ask questions about him, I saw him just appear out of the mist in the back of the courtyard at a table. He just stared at me. I went through so much havoc. Those spirits follow you and destroy everything you touch. I was in a car accident where I was hit from behind. I had a female Hispanic witness; however, the men who hit me were in a Breuner's Furniture truck and they were white, and we were in Scottsdale. So, even though my car was kicked across the light out into the street, I was dazed but I knew I couldn't leave my car out in traffic because my children were in the back seat. I went to court. It took three years and I received very little, especially after the doctor and lawyer bills. The accident caused permanent damage. Prior to that, I was off from work due to the accident, wore a brace, and had no car since it eventually broke down. Due to time off from work, I was late on my rent one month. I tried to pay half of it and pay the other later, but the rental office just filed eviction papers. They wouldn't even accept me paying any part of the rent. I realized they never really wanted me to live there. I was railroaded in the court. The judge in Scottsdale was prejudiced and heartless.

Even amid all of the chaos, God was still making a way for me. A man left a flyer on my door. I called him. I didn't know anything about buying a house and surely didn't know what to bid on a house. I had no clue about what a HUD home was either. He gave me the keys and told me to go look at several house and find one I was interested in. When we came to the house in Mesa, the kids and I knelt down and prayed and asked God for the house. The realtor bid on the home for us. We won the bid. I put up $500 earnest money that I eventually got back. I bought another car but I owed money on it. But just like the Hebrews who never learned their lesson, neither did I. The Hebrews had witnessed God's mighty hand, how God freed them from Egypt, fed them with manna from Heaven in the wilderness, protected them from Pharaoh's army by staying them with fire, and opening up the Red Sea so they could cross over safely. They witnessed all of this yet they murmured and complained and sinned still. I was that same way. I continued in sin with the witch. However, it was there that he actually confirmed that he was a witch, that is, a white witch. He said he used his powers for good. My aunt told me to stop seeing him, to burn up or throw out anything he had given me, and to anoint myself and my children, and my entire house with oil. She told me to go through and pray. I did this. I was determined not to allow these spirits to control my life. I did see him again after that, but not socially. I just happened to see him at a convenience store. He said, *"Hello."* I said *"Hello."* There was nothing else said and I never saw him again. I quit Motorola to go to school full-time. I was determined to get my degree. I realized that I needed that piece of paper to go further in my career.

Sometimes parents tell their children that, *"All you have to do is go to school. I have to go to work."* I'm sure people don't realize how mentally draining it is to go to school. When you work, most of the time your day is done, that is, unless you bring your work home with you – not a good idea. When you go to school, you have studying and homework after the classes are done. You have papers to write. Unfortunately, I've never been out of work for too long a time. I've always worked at temporary agencies. My income changed dramatically since I no longer had the Motorola income. I voluntarily surrendered my car. I was instrumental in getting HUD to reduce my home payments through a special program. I would pay for this later. It didn't dawn on me that they were "taking" all of that money with interest to the backend of my loan. In addition, I applied for scholarships left and right. Writing has always been my strength. As long as the evaluators were unable to see that I was a black woman I could make a good impression. During that year, I acquired 10 scholarships, one of which was an ASU Regent's Scholarship. I was pre-med and majoring in Chemistry. This helped me win one of the Black Women's Task Force scholarships. I was also non-assuming and brow-beaten by this time.

My experience at ASU was a rocky one to say the least. I was thankful for the Re-Entry Center located in the lower level of the Memorial Union – the "MU" they called it. There were times when they might as well have been saying "FU." The English teachers were my favorite. I had some good ones. In fact, the English & Humanities Department and Foreign Language Dept. were the only ones who cared whether or not you attended each class. The Math and Sciences teachers were always so busy. They taught in lecture halls that sometimes comprised 100 students. I managed to survive although I felt alone most of the time. There were few teachers and students that looked like me. I was able to acquire a weird set of hearing aids when it was determined that I had a hearing impairment. This must have stemmed from the time I tried to throw a firecracker on my dog when I was a kid. It kept going out and I had to try to relight it, but the wick kept getting shorter and shorter. It ended up popping in my face. In addition to this, I spent all those years at Unicorn Systems Co. where I had do transcription most of the day.

Since I was pre-med, I decided to volunteer at what was then known as Desert Samaritan Hospital (now Banner) in Mesa. It was right down the street from my house and I wanted to get a feel for what doctors, nurses, and health care staff dealt with in their careers. Over a two-year period, I volunteered in Emergency, Medical Records, and Long-Term Care. The Emergency Room was the hardest. I cleaned up the emergency room after I learned that I didn't have the stamina for standing on my feet for long hours at a time. Therefore, becoming an RN or surgeon was definitely out of the question. I learned that the weekend was the popular time when most people got into car accidents, committed domestic violence, and tried to commit suicide.

We had a young white girl about 16 years old who had swallowed too many pills. I don't remember what kind of pills they were, but I do remember assisting the doctor and nurse who had pumped her stomach with charcoal. Her lips and tongue were blackened from the experience. I asked her if I could get her anything. She said she was fine. She talked with me briefly later. I still couldn't understand how anyone only 16 years old could have a life that was so horrible they wanted to die. I learned later that she really just wanted the attention. It was a cry for help. It was during this hospital volunteer experience that I could see the correlation between the physically sick who need a hospital and a physician to promote physical and mental healing, and the sin sick who need the church and a pastor to promote spiritual and mental and emotional healing. In the Long Term Care unit I would play "at" the keyboard, but the elderly residents thought it was the greatest thing they had ever heard. I would sometimes read the Bible to them, and other times just sit there and listen to them while they told me things that sometimes had no beginning or end or did not make sense. It didn't matter. Some of them had no one to visit them. It made them happy just to have company. I wish I could say that I'm a saint, but that's not true. I could only stand this for so long.

Single women are so vulnerable. I guess another word for this is "human." We are all sexual beings, but reason, logic, and conscience set us apart from the animal kingdom. Some would say we evolved, but I'm not a Darwinian. I know it is because God made us in his own image. He did put within us that sexual drive because this is what keeps us from extinction. I had a crush on my male Spanish teacher. I would sometimes bring my daughter with me to classes. She used to like to rummage through my handbag. He playfully yelled at her, *"Get out of your mother's purse!"* She was startled. He and the class laughed, and I had to console her. I found myself with a crush on my teacher. It wasn't until this day that I remember why. He reminded me of a boy named Carlos in my neighborhood when I grew up in Compton. We played this kissing game. I thought he was so cute. I would discover that my teacher was very cute. It was not until I'd embarrassed myself by writing him a little love note that I learned he was gay. I don't know if I was blinded by his good looks because I could swear his mannerisms were more noticeable once he told me was gay than they had been before. Perhaps I thought it was his Cuban way. I did well in my Spanish class, anyway.

Some students know from Day 1 what they want as a major and pursue it. Some of us flounder around, and some of us declare a new major, if not every year, every semester. I did well in my classes but I didn't like

Biology because I was forced to learn and accept Evolution as though it were fact, even though in reality it has not been proven. I knew that pursuing a career in medicine would mean that I would one day have to take Zoology and be forced to skin a cat and dissect it. Neither or these prospects delighted me. Also, one of my classmates who was pre-med, already knew that his career was pre-made and prepared for him. His father was a doctor. In fact, he was 17 years old and making $20 per hour on a part-time basis. This was almost 20 years ago. He told me he was a Christian, but I also discovered he was gay. We were friends but we agreed to disagree on this subject, mostly because he was unsure of this part of his life. He was just surprised that I didn't think God approved of it. I pointed him to the Scriptures and we left it at that.

I knew that I would never be a white male, nor did I want to be. However, I sure wished I had their opportunities. I didn't realize it back then, but it would be through appearing as a victim because of their sexual sin and likening their plight to that of slavery, that the white man would stab affirmative action in the back, kick Martin Luther King's struggle to the curb, laugh and blaspheme in the face of true Bible believing and Christ-serving Christians, and would emerge victorious to become part of the "federally protected class." Yes, I said SIN. God calls it sin and I serve Him. If it looks like a duck and quacks like a duck, guess what, it's a duck.

I decided to test further whether or not I would be cut out to be a doctor. In one semester, I took Biology, Bio-chemistry, Physics, and English. The kicker came when it was time for finals. I took all of them in the same day because that's the day they were all scheduled. I didn't find out until later that when you had more than two in the same day, you could have the others rescheduled. My Physics final was the last. By the time I got to it, my brain had already left the building. I hit a wall and had nothing left to give. I stared at my paper and wondered why in the world I was sitting in that classroom. I had an "A" going into the final. When I got the postcard from my professor, he had put an "F" with a "?" for the Final Grade; however, I received a "C" in the class. In my mind, I would never be able to cut it in medical school. I knew they were under constant pressure. I knew they had to go through internship and residency. I also knew it would be a grueling experience. You had to either have the heart and drive for this type of field or the heart and drive to make good money. I had neither. In addition, I was more into holistic healing through herbs. I knew that doctors were trained to prescribe medication. I knew that surgeons received 10 times their normal salary when they performed a surgery. I knew that this field was not for me. Had I known about naturopathic medicine at the time, I may have pursued it. Unfortunately, I was unaware of it. Besides, God consoled my heart. He showed me clear as day that I would be a "healer of hearts."

Working for temporary agencies just seemed like it was a part of my life, which is why I would later do temporary employment through my for-profit business. Everything you do in your life is training for something else later on. Agencies loved using me because I could type close to 100 words per minute. These were my piano fingers at work. My music created words on a page or created spreadsheets. Like the apostle Paul, I would always have that talent on which to fall to provide for my family and myself. Even today, if I had to, I can get a job working temporarily doing this kind of work. It wouldn't be as readily available due to the multitude of outsourcing, but where there's a will, believe me, there is a way.

I was placed on a temporary assignment at Philips, Inc. The only thing I knew about them up to this point was that they made screwdrivers and light bulbs. I always heard my father say that he needed "a Philips screwdriver" for whatever he was fixing or repairing. It was a small company in Tempe. It was a two-man office who were hardly ever there. Natalie was in charge. She was married and had a son. She seemed nice enough and generous, but little did I know that she would be suspected of stealing from the company. When my daughter came to pick me up from work, especially on a Saturday, Natalie gave us things like Calistoga sodas and a large cookbook. I remember riding with her to go run an errand one day. She was definitely a "multi-tasker." That was the first time I'd ever seen anyone drive a car, talk on the cell phone, and write a check at the same time. I promised myself I would never get into another car with her again.

I am so glad that, although I'm not perfect and do make mistakes, God is always in control and is the head of my life. He watches over me and protects me. I see his divine hand during that time. Natalie wanted to ask me something. She started the sentence, but it was as if she caught herself and never finished saying what she wanted to say. She said, *"You know you can make a lot of money..."* I thought she was talking about doing temporary work for the company. I thought maybe she could get them to extend my assignment, or better yet, maybe even hire me. Silly me, this could not have been further from what she had in mind. After I was no longer working there, I got a call from an attorney who was "investigating Natalie's case." Apparently, she had been stealing the company blind. She'd bought thousands and thousands of dollars worth of merchandise on the company. I guess this included computers, electronics equipment, and so many other items. I couldn't believe it! Now I knew what she'd meant by "you can make a lot of money." They asked me what I knew. I told them, even though I didn't know very much. I prayed for her. I never found out what happened. I was concerned about her son more than anything.

Then came several assignments through another agency based out of Phoenix. They seemed kind of "ho-hum" about me until I tested at a typing speed of 102 words per minute with three errors. They placed me on different assignments at Motorola, Inc. They were still into semiconductors at that time. I worked in several different departments in Chandler. I learned a great deal and acquired more computer experience – this time with the Linux and Unix Operating Systems. I was always the central hub, the coordinator – actually a "glorified" receptionist and secretary. I ran a lot of errands also. I did my work, was innovative, and was a social butterfly. They liked me everywhere I went. However, I began to realize that my life and experience would be similar metaphorically to that of the prophets and Jesus. People loved me at first and were amazed at all the "miracles" I could perform in my job. They loved being fed with the "fishes and loaves of bread" and the "healing" that I provided to make their departments run more efficiently and make the company lots of money. Because of my faith in God, I was a light in a dark place. I've begun to learn that White people have a "place" for me. They don't care what I do or accomplish, as long as I stay in that place to which they have relegated for me and/or reserved for me. Because I am God's anointed and His appointed, I don't fit into this place. They soon find that there is so much more to me. They began to feel threatened by my talents and abilities. As usual, it's the enemy who infiltrates their minds and causes them to feel resentful and/or suspicious of me and my motives. They always put mechanisms into place to make sure I don't prosper. To my detriment, they intentionally hold me to a higher standard than they hold for themselves. They have this unwritten protocol to which they want you to adhere. It doesn't matter that you don't know what that protocol is until you've done or said the wrong thing, that is, according to them. I see this spirit in White men who are in leadership positions more than I have seen it in White women, but then, I don't know everyone. That unwritten protocol says you're not supposed to initiate an interaction with individuals who are on a "higher level" than you. This "higher level" refers to economic status, company title, community title, and celebrity status. I respect everyone as a human being, not because of a title, position, or how much money they have. They are human beings, not God. They are no better than I am. A lot of times they are not as good a person as I am. A lot of times, they feel they don't have to be. It is for this reason that sometimes my temporary employment contract was not extended or renewed.

They placed me at Intel Corporation. I assisted with the company volunteer program. However, most of the time, I created and revised spreadsheets. I worked there for a total of one day short of six months. After four months into the project, the temporary agency placed another White man to work with me in the same department. There was a small amount of training I provided to him and to bring him up to speed. I kept wondering why they brought him in when it didn't seem as though there was enough work for just me. Little did

I know he was there to replace me. I thought it was odd that they invited him to a baby shower of one of the employees. It was held at the office. I found out about it by accident, bought a gift, and went to the baby shower. They gave me looks to indicate that I wasn't expected. However, no one said anything. It wasn't until the temp agency told me that my contract was not going to be renewed that I understood what was going on. The young man was a nice enough person and from what I could tell, he was also a Christian. However, I also realized that he was a friend or a relative of one of the employees at Intel.

I was so disheartened that, again, this travesty and unfairness had been done to me. I decided to leave one day before the assignment was over. In my realm of thinking, they had already told me they no longer needed me, so what difference would one day make? I would learn later that they can treat you anyway they want to, that they expect you to take it, and not say anything about it. I made a point to make sure I finished up anything on which I was working. I left a note for my supervisor. I called my agency to tell them what was going on. I was not physically ill. I was emotionally ill from how I'd been treated. Apparently, no one cared. I left my keys with the Intel supervisor. I left everything in order.

When I tried to apply for unemployment, I was denied because my agency protested it. I couldn't believe it. I'd worked for them almost six months. I'd paid into my unemployment. Besides, I'd been working for so many years. Now, I needed that money to take care of my family. I tried to appeal the decision. Of course, this was done in Mesa Court with a mediator and they ruled in favor of the agency. I was so dejected. I have come to believe that Arizona is not a good place for a Black woman to live, unless she is retired and already married. This is definitely not the land of opportunity for us. A good friend of mine, who lives in California, once told me that I've "been rowing upstream with one oar for a long time." She was referring to my experience and trials in Arizona.

So, I found myself on public assistance for a while. I got just enough cash and food stamps to exist on. I believe going to school was also a survival technique. I could get student loans to sustain my family while trying to find employment. I remember being hired by two gentlemen at Bank of America in Mesa. For the most part it was an evening job doing cold-call telemarketing. I had a script that they'd given me. They didn't mind that my daughter came with me at night. It didn't take long before I realized that I didn't like working at night because I'm a morning person, and that telemarketing was not for me. This was my second try at telemarketing and I virtually hated it. In fact, I've learned that I don't really like marketing a product in which I don't believe, know about, or feel helps the person to whom I'm selling. The deciding moment came when I was making a call to one of their potential clients. I hadn't realized at first what I said, *"Hello, Mrs. Butterball?"* My daughter started laughing. I started into the first words of my script, when I started laughing. I had to hang up the phone. Unfortunately, I'd already told her I was from Bank of America. The next day I told my two bosses that I was quitting.

I remember applying for positions at ASU during the time I was getting my bachelor's degree. I felt work-study would help me. I never got a call from anyone. I had an article published in the *Arizona Informant*. It was a few moments of glory that would lead to long term agony. Not only could I not get work study jobs, but I tried to get ASU's periodical to publish one or two of my poems. I would submit them, but never see them in print or hear anything about them. When I finally confronted the editors to find out what happened to them. The two young white college students responsible for intake of contributions, just laughed, and said, *"What poems???"* It was then that I first understood how young white people could get jobs that I couldn't, and would also be allowed to have control and independence to my detriment. In fact, as I write this, there is a young person who works for the *Casa Grande Dispatch* who interviewed me for an article she was doing about adult education and employment. I discovered that she was not an intern but an employee and she was still a student seeking her A.A. degree. I am a firm believer that, even with my degrees, my experience, and as a published author, they would not hire me. I've found this city to be extremely racist.

Timing is a great asset, if you have it. I don't. It would have been nice to have been employed with ASU during the time I was getting my bachelor's degree. I could have attended classes at a discount and saved owing so much money in student loans. How I got the job was a fluke in the first place. I remember sending in my resume. Linda, who was the ASU Foundation Administrative Assistant to Lonnie, was the person who called me in for an interview. I was supposed to interview with Chuck, but he apparently had food poisoning the day before, and so Linda interviewed me. It would not be until a year after I was hired that Linda confessed to me that Chuck did not want to hire me. He did not feel I had enough background in Finance. Linda told him that a person with a bachelor's degree in English could fit in anywhere. Not to mention that the position was a secretary position – duh!

So, upon L's recommendation, Chuck interviewed me, and I was hired. I cannot, to this day, believe that I worked there for three years. I never once received a pay increase. Everyone is nice when you first start working somewhere. While everyone else had to have assigned parking or park a mile off campus, the ASU Foundation was housed in an old donated bank building. We had our own parking. The building was one level and centrally located off College and University. I had my own cubicle and I was happy – for a while. I was over qualified for the position, but when they finished with me, they tried to make it seem as though I was not even qualified for that position.

Somehow you think working for a different entity will be different, but somehow, it's always the same. I was still living in West Mesa in the same condominium. I was still plagued by the same entanglement with what I thought was a good ministry in South Phoenix at Christian New Life. As usual, I learned new software programs, a bit more computer hardware, but had to deal with the same old evil people. The Bible is absolutely right when it says "their words are smooth as butter, but there is war in their hearts." For a long time the receptionist position was one where the secretaries oversaw. When the receptionist was out, the temporary agency was called upon to supply a substitute. None of the secretaries were ever asked to fill in for the receptionist. That is, until my supervisor appointed me supervisor over the receptionist.

I'd been in this supervisory role before. It was nothing new. Not sure what they intended, but I was determined to be real supervisor. The receptionist resented reporting to me. I'm certain it had nothing to do with my being a Black woman. My supervisor did not like the fact that I would take off days when he was not going to be there. There was not a great deal of work to do during that particular week, and I saw no point in just babysitting a phone. He thought otherwise, and, apparently, so did the other secretaries. In my mind, this job was just an interim on to what God had really planned for me to do at the ASU Foundation. I worked really hard. My supervisor had me transcribe his voicemail messages. This was not easy for me since I have a hearing impairment. Sometimes I had to listen to the messages two or three times to get every word. However, I accomplished my goal. I attended the Board meetings and took the minutes to be typed up at the next meeting. I even prepared the materials for the meetings. It was a lot of work. Granted, there were a couple of times I was not there and thought everything was taken care of, when my supervisor informed me that things were screwed up and the other secretaries had to help him put the packets together. He did this way ahead of schedule, thinking I was not going to be there to meet the deadline. I now know that Dale, his male assistant, was sabotaging me. The Devil will always set up camp close by me. He seeks only to kill, steal, and destroy.

I remember writing a poem for my supervisor for his birthday. I created public folders in Outlook and found ways to reduce the use of paper. Among the many other tasks I performed for my supervisor, I washed his windows. I was the butt of office jokes because of this. I didn't care. I saw myself as a servant, not to my supervisor, but to God. The Bible tells us to do "all as unto the Lord and not as unto men." It says we should not be "man pleasers, but pleasers of God." In every job I believe we can learn something. There should always be some type of skill or knowledge that you acquire to help you prosper and move forward. I am grateful to the ASU

Foundation only because it is there I learned how to start my nonprofit organization. I did not know at the time what it would become or even the full ramifications, but I knew it was from God. Before I received my 501(c)3, I was able to use another organization as the fiscal agent and acquire equipment and furniture. I even acquired a couple of pieces of equipment from the ASU Foundation that was donated, but my supervisor and his assistant would rather have seen the equipment stuffed away in a dungeon somewhere or given to anyone else except me. I didn't know it at the time, but this was among several strikes against me in my supervisor's eyes.

The older I get, I realize that living in Arizona is incredibly difficult for a dark-skinned Black woman who is industrious and intelligent. Things really came to a head when I took my position seriously as supervisor over the receptionist. I was over-qualified already, but it became apparent that my supervisor wanted me to just fill in when the receptionist was absent. None of the other administrative assistants had to do this. I would do the same thing they did when the receptionist was out: I would call the temporary service. My supervisor did not like this. I knew that I was receiving different treatment because of who I was and what I looked like. In addition, my supervisor did not like the fact that I gave the receptionist a performance review and recommended to him that she received a raise in pay. In fact, he was furious.

Everyone was happy when I was the office clown, made jokes, and laughed at everything they did. No one wanted me to think on my own. My supervisor wanted me to just sit and answer phones, type when necessary, file, and transcribe his voicemails. When I think back, I could have brought a lawsuit for a lot of things, one of which would have come under the American Disabilities Act, since I had a hearing impairment, but I digress.

I never received a raise during the whole time I worked there. My performance review was awful. My supervisor made it seem as though I should never have been hired in the first place. I knew I was being treated unjustly. In fact, what he'd done had not come as a surprise. I had prayed and prayed the week before. I already knew that when God was ready for me to leave He would show me. God impressed upon my mind that if my supervisor did give me a performance review like the one I did get, I should let him know that "he would suffer a loss in his life." I knew that God meant that my supervisor would lose something of value that he owned. I wasn't sure what it was. I thought maybe it was me; however, I'm sure he didn't see me as valuable. My supervisor must have thought I was talking about something physically or terrible happening to him that I or someone was going to cause. He brought in an investigator. I thought it was funny because I couldn't believe he thought I would try to hurt him. I washed the man's windows at the office for God's sake! I told them that I was a minister. However, I started remembering the incident I relayed to everyone, including my supervisor, about how the bicycle policemen had pulled me over because I didn't see a stop sign that was only on one corner of the street. I had travelled that street so many times, so the sign must have been new. I noticed that several people were also failing to stop while the policeman was writing me a ticket. It was two weeks until Christmas. I had worked late. My daughter was in the car and we hadn't had dinner yet. I was so tired and irritable. I made a comment to him about "meeting a quota." Apparently, they get real irate about this, which makes me believe it's true.

I noticed why people were not seeing the sign and I tried to tell him. He was ignoring me and told me to move out. I said, *"Will you shut up and listen to me?"* Not the right thing to say. He grabbed me out of the car, almost breaking my seat belt, and threw me up on the back of the hood. My daughter was about to get out when he told her to stay in there or she would be going to jail. My daughter just wanted to make sure I was all right. I just relaxed so he would not have any reason to become more violent. They called for backup. I just sat on the ground and started singing Christian songs. When the police cars (two of them) arrived, they couldn't help but find the whole thing amusing. I told them what happened. I received another ticket for failing to obey a police officer. I reported the whole thing to my pastor who was vice mayor of Mesa at the time and the minister in our church who was a police officer in Mesa. The pastor said, *"They don't really know how to handle us."* I paid the small fine in court even though I was tempted to sue. I really don't like lawsuits.

It was this incident that my supervisor was remembering. I'm sure he thought I had been violent, but he remembered well that I had told the officer to "shut up." When I came in the next morning, his assistant (farmer in the dell) was more than happy to tell me that the campus police officers were there for me. They told me to get my things and they were escorting me out. They asked if I had any weapons. I showed them my Bible and told them that this was my weapon. My daughter had just dropped me off at work. I had to call her to come right back to pick me up. he couldn't believe what had happened.

Once again, I found myself filing charges with EEOC, to no avail. If I were to give anyone living in

Arizona who has been racially discriminated against and is a minority, I would tell them to get a high-priced lawyer and sue. This is the only way you'll ever win. I still received my paycheck, which was very small and insignificant. Funny thing, they were supposed to be doing an investigation. I had several people in the office tell me over the phone that they thought it was ridiculous that my supervisor felt as though I had threatened him. After about a month or so, amazingly, I was asked to come back to my position. Apparently, after they'd changed my position and prevented me from having access to public folders, my supervisor was no longer in fear for his life. It was safe now. I knew exactly what they were doing. I had information on them. I had also told them that their Happy Hours should not have been considered "Business Expenses." My supervisor was just trying to teach me a lesson. Once again, the white "massa" wanted me to cry "Toby." I resigned without going back in. They had degraded and humiliated me. I couldn't believe they would do that to me after all I had done there. This scenario would be continually repeated while working in Arizona. I decided to pursue the teaching field.

I discovered that I only needed a bachelor's degree to become a substitute teacher. I worked for Mesa Public Schools, Chandler Unified School District, Gilbert Public Schools, and Maricopa Regional School District. One substitute position was more memorable than others. I had real good rapport with the students in the third grade class. We had fun and they learned something. I was usually called in at the last minute and did not have time to look over the lesson beforehand. It had been a long while since I had studied elementary school level language arts, let alone teach it. I was not given time to review. However, the same teacher wanted to use me again. Everyone was happy until one little boy decided he didn't want me to tell him what to do. He lost out on one of the activities. Apparently, he'd told his parents about it. Also, I remember the other teachers coming through my classroom a few times as if they were checking up on me. To make matters worse, during an assembly I talked with a couple of the teachers and told them about my writing.

Before my paranoia could take hold, lo and behold, the next day of my substitute assignment, the principal sat in my classroom. He made me nervous and I couldn't really do a good job. I knew he was there for a self-fulfilling prophecy. He had never greeted me and had never even given me a second thought, but here he was in the classroom. His comment was that he wanted to make sure the students had a good handle on the lesson. First of all, he must not have a lot to do as principal of the school. Second of all, substitutes are expected to pretty much babysit. However, his racism was showing. He wanted to make sure that I would not be used again at their school. I never got called back.

I did get a temporary assignment working for Thomas J. Papas Middle School in Tempe. These were students who were homeless. I enjoyed working with them because they really seemed to want to learn. The assignment was a short one. After this, I was sent way out to Estrella Mountain High School. Maricopa County was in the process of giving over jurisdiction to the tribe. It happened to be a K-12 charter school for Native American students. The classes were ungraded. I taught a class with all age groups. I remember talking to one of the female 9-year-olds on the playground. She told me there was nothing wrong with smoking marijuana, that she did this with her tribe, especially during their rituals. I was shocked, mainly because she was only 9 years old.

I told her that I did not want to disrespect her family traditions, but that she needed to get a little more information on the subject. I cautioned her that marijuana can have devastating effects on young people. It can zap their motivation and cause sterility in males. She just sort of laughed, but at least the seed was planted so that she would question and seek answers for herself.

I remember one older student who would just stand outside by the wall during lunchtime. He never said anything and he never ate lunch. I tried to talk to him but he did not respond. The most devastating experience was a 9-year-old boy who was in my class during the time we were studying Math. I gave them an assignment and he threw his book on the floor. My first thought was to get on him to pick it up. I decided instead to focus on the students who were working. When he saw that I wasn't going to address what he did, he picked up the book and started working. I watched him leave when class was over. He was going across the way with a friend of his. This was on a Friday. The following Monday I learned that he had hung himself. I was told that his birthday was a month ago. This was during the early part of December. His brother received a walkman for his birthday. Apparently my student had always wanted a walkman. On the reservation they could not afford very much. This surprised me because I knew how much money the casinos took in. I couldn't believe that some of them lived in such poverty, or what looked like poverty. My student did not really want to die; he wanted attention; he wanted the pain in his life to go away. I know this because I was told that he had serious scratch marks all on the sides of his neck as if he tried to remove the homemade noose but was unable to do so. I was unable to attend the entire funeral. Since I was new and only a temporary, I had to stay behind with the other students. They did, however, allow me to take a card to the family at lunch time to the church where the funeral was being held. I saw so many of his male relatives leaving in shackles. These men were supposed to be there for him. These men were supposed to be his mentors. They were not around when he needed them the most.

I got hired at East Valley Middle School on a long-term substitute assignment through Maricopa Regional Schools. East Valley Middle School was a challenge for me and I learned a great deal there. I remember when the school was closing that one of the female white teachers received a grant to work from her home with the same kinds of students. This started my mind to thinking about grants and how you could possibly get one to teach. In the meantime, I was lucky to be working.

The other important event during that time was Halle Berry winning the Academy Award for Best Actress in Monster's Ball. I had never the seen the movie, but one of the male teachers commented about her raunchy sex scene and the fact that she cried profusely and her makeup didn't run, not even once. I did see the movie later after that and wished I hadn't. I was so ashamed that this was the movie for which she got recognition. They said Angela Bassett turned down the role. It's always the way: they slight us and then back track and give us what we should have had a million years ago, but this time they give it for something that does not truly represent your talents. For example, when Denzel Washington received an Academy Award for his role in Training Day – this was an awful movie. However, Tom Hanks, Meryl Streep, and Nicole Kidman, for example, get great roles to play. Their acting is no better than many female and male black actresses, but they get great parts. Their movie roles mean something and they are known for these parts. This is why Halle has never had a meaningful or what they would call an award-winning performance since that time. She's a wonderful actress and is still treated with such disrespect. Everybody talks about the kiss that Adrien Brody gave Halle Berry after she presented his Oscar. This was degrading and disrespectful. He would never have done this to a white woman who was the previous Academy Award winner who had just presented him with an Oscar.

This brings me to cultural diversity and sensitivity when it comes to how black women are treated, in the workplace, and outside of the workplace: the negative image of Sapphire and Aunt Jemima. We were always one or the other. If you were dark-skinned and not seen as having so-called "white" features, then you were treated as an Aunt Jemima. In my previous years, I was seen as the humorous sapphire because I was thin and young. As I started to age, I was now the humorous Aunt Jemima. Sun Valley High School was not known for its cultural sensitivity. Oh, they considered themselves culturally diverse, but I discovered otherwise. I was hired to work in the middle school section that was just beginning. I was going to be paid a good salary because I could teach both Math and English. The former teacher at East Valley lauded the principal of Sun Valley High School. I would find out later that most of the white employers in Arizona are, for the most part, racists.

It is amazing to me that a great deal of the white people in Arizona would not consider themselves as racists. Yet, the remarks and treatment is not even covert; it is usually overt. I did not make it past the cut through orientation at Sun Valley. When I think back, I realized I should have been a good little "N---girl" and held my peace. I realize that I was too outspoken. I was never really received well from the other teachers or staff. One of the English teachers, who had been there for a long time, found out that I majored in English. She kept questioning to find out who my favorite author was. I started to tell her that I was, but it would not have satisfied her. I read prolifically when I was younger and when I had to in college. Now I read the Bible more than anything. I didn't like reading fiction anymore. I had the feeling she was trying to find out if I really did have a degree in English. When you are a black woman you are never given the benefit of the doubt as white women are. You have to prove yourself and you have to be two or three times as good. This gets tremendously annoying after awhile.

During teacher in-service I made the mistake of suggesting to the principal that the school needed diversity training. I was sure of this after one of the teachers was "asking a question" and repeatedly used the "N-word." To avoid what could have been a potential lawsuit, the principal had the teacher apologize to me. However, not too many days after that, I was told that there was not enough funding for me to continue employment with the school. This was really no surprise to me.

A friend of mine told me about a new charter school in South Phoenix. It was unique because it was run by a black man. It was supposed to be innovative. What amazes me is that my friend had no degree and did not have the teaching background that I had, yet she managed to get the job as a teacher with a better classroom than I had and was paid the same salary as me. Because she was articulate and attractive, she wielded people, mostly men, to think and act in her favor. I always envied this about her. Most people don't see me as attractive, I have dark skin, and I always have to prove myself before I am well received. My friend had set the stage for me, so I thought. She told the owner and operator about me. The school was named after its owner: Charles Wilson Academy. Apparently he was a pastor and had a church in Peoria. You could tell he and his staff were feeling their way around. I was hired to teach Third Grade. I was told that I would be teaching the older grade levels later. I discovered that Mr. Wilson had plans for me not to teach but to research and write grants. I loved the third graders. It's usually the same with all students: they really don't care how much you know until they first know how much you care. I would give them lots of hugs and treats. They loved me and cried when I had to go a different position.

My friend's classroom had a bathroom inside the classroom. It had nice tile and was readily accessible to the other facilities. My classroom had a dirt floor. Everything was substandard and the students, I would discover, were students with learning disabilities and had not been identified. I'm not sure why my life is always a hard road, but I deal with it. In addition, at the beginning my friend intimated that she wanted us to work together on lesson plans. I realized that, once again, I was about to be used. Once again, I would do a lot of work while someone else reaped the benefits. I decided not to help her. No matter, she found someone else who was happy to do it: the teacher's aide. Supposedly, I had a teacher's aide. Naturally, she was always absent.

I thought that because finances were scarce, teachers and staff had to buy their own copy paper and recycle what they used. This was my first experience with recycling and I found it to be extremely effective and useful. We had staff meetings on Wednesdays. I never actually felt like a part of the staff. I felt disjointed even though the group was predominantly African American. Mr. Wilson's wife was the vice principal. Supposedly, she evaluated my class one day. I was taken from the classroom and assigned as a grant writer. I worked with an agency with whom he had contracted for the 21st Century Community Learning Center grant. In addition, I was to meet with other agencies and research out other grant opportunities for the school. I resented the fact that I was not in class with my third graders, but it had its purpose and I learned a great deal. I interviewed a woman in downtown Phoenix who had a charter school. I found her because of an article I'd read about her. She was the founder of the Birthing Project. I visited her school and was impressed with the painting she had on the wall with the words, *"It takes two people to have a child, but it takes a whole village to raise a child."* She talked with me, told me about her school, and gave me a few leads and pointers with regards to grant opportunities. I also met with one of the school's partners, an adult community center down the street from the school. We usually have no idea how people we meet or places with whom we come into contact will re-surface in the future or how they will fit in with you later in life. This would be the case with me a few years later.

You can tell when things are not quite right, but may be unable at the time to put your finger on the problem. I already had my own sole proprietorship at that time. I saw more and more that Mr. Wilson expected me to provide these services to the school for free under the guise of my new position. This, coupled with the fact that I discovered my friend was being paid the same amount that I was receiving, was too much for me to bear. What's amazing is that there was an incident involving her son whereby she ended up resigning. I too resigned. Mr. Wilson contracted with me to do their 501(c)3 for the school and for another private foundation connected in some way with the school. I did both. This gave me a great deal of information I would use later to apply for my own charter school. I discovered later that the school was closed by the Charter School Board because they had apparently misappropriated funds and/or were in non-compliance with various rules and regulations. This left a bad taste in the mouths of those who had felt hopeful about the first African American-owned charter school in Arizona.

I was still substitute teaching here and there; however, I managed to get a long-term assignment at Lone Cactus charter school way up north. It was a long drive but you do what you have to do. I had my own classroom and I would be teaching Math. I was thrown into the position at the last minute. I had to do lesson plans for the following Monday so I came in on the weekend to prepare everything. The students were predominantly white and it was a closed campus with barbed wire. They could not leave the campus at lunch time and the staff supervised them while we ate our lunch. My first classroom was in the bungalow. We had a buzzer whereby we could call for Security if we needed them. I gave the students my all like I always do; however, most of them were bent on not liking me. What was interesting is that I was told that the students liked the teacher before me and she was also a black woman. I later discovered that the teacher never gave them anything of difficulty to work on; she never challenged their minds. She told jokes and played around with them. I, on the other hand, was a bit too serious for them. They gave me a hard time no matter what good I did for them. One student even commented that I thought they should bend down and kiss my feet. This surprised me. I knew she said it out of guilt because they really had no reason to dislike me. I was not their "buffoon" or their "Aunt Jemima." I was a firm disciplinarian, which is what they needed. A great deal of them were in this alternative school because they had been disobedient to parents and authorities, used drugs, committed crimes, and kicked out of other traditional schools. However, like I said, I was teaching Math, a subject I love. The teachers had an intercom in the room whereby they could call the security guard if they needed help with an unruly or disobedient student. When I was first at the school I had to call them a great number of times; however, the frequency decreased as time went on. It wasn't that the students were obedient; I just got used to them and learned how to deal with them. I found most of them were spoiled and came from well-to-do homes. They were privileged and chose to disobey their parents.

The students loved the English teacher. She was white, blonde, and thin. She was the object of their affection, and I was the Aunt Jemima who was a disciplinarian. The fact that I was a Christian woman didn't help matters. I remember one of the skinheads told me he was going to put a bomb under my car. I told him to "go ahead and try it." They never did anything. The only one of them who was in my class told the principal that he did not want to be in my classroom, so they moved him to another classroom. At the end of the school year, he asked the blonde English teacher to talk to me about helping him to win a $10,000 scholarship. When she came to me, I was adamant that I would in no way assist any student who felt they could not stand to be in my classroom. The subject was dropped.

The principal told me one day that she was having a hard time filling up my classes because the students did want to take my class. It should not have mattered if the students liked me or not; they needed to learn the subject matter. However, this principal catered to them because she wanted to be liked. I remember they hired a black male teacher. He was in his early 20's and seemed pretty cocky. He told me how he knew was "the name of the game" because black men had grown in popularity and were sought out. He was right. Strange how the black man was sought out and revered and a black woman like me was ostracized. However, what was even more amazing was that he knew this and it didn't bother him in the least that I was treated the way I was. My assignment was a long-term temporary assignment that I thought would turn into a permanent position with Maricopa County Regional. However, I was told that because I hadn't completed my certification I would not be eligible for a permanent position. And, of course, during the next school year, they didn't have an assignment for me (temporary of otherwise). God still has His hand in everything that happens. There is a scripture that says, "All things work together for good for those that love God and called according to His purpose" (Romans 8:28). All experiences either make you or break you. You have to transcend the negative experiences and go forward. So, forward I went.

By now, I was focusing more on my own business. I have to say that in the past I just haven't had the right timing with the right services and/or products with the right staff. It would be many years later that I would learn that unless you are in tuned with God and seek His direction and guidance, you will never have the right timing. But, there I was: F.A.I.T.H. (Fast And Indispensable Temporary Help) Services – doing temporary employment. I'd worked for so many temporary help agencies and they'd helped me so much, especially when no one else in Arizona would recognize my abilities through my resume of education and experience. So, I wanted to help other individuals by placing them on temporary assignments. The problem was I discovered my weakness: marketing. It wasn't that I didn't know how to do it. I'd studied prolifically. It wasn't that I didn't have some funds for it. The problem was, and I didn't know this at the time, I wasn't just marketing a service. I was marketing myself. I found myself in the same predicament as when I was working for others: people were rejecting me. It was only after much painstaking and they actually saw what I could do and benefited by what I did, that they were surprised and grateful. However, they never referred anyone. Also, I was at fault because I failed to ask for referrals. I was in a catch-22. People buy from people they like. This is also true with hiring. Despite all of your education, background, skills, and abilities – employers hire people they like or know. It's plain and simple. The problem is I am an unwanted commodity: a Christian Black woman who is dark-skinned, moles on her face, over 50, intelligent, and assertive. Most of the time I'm so busy doing things that I don't take time out to tell people what I'm doing.

Back then, in 1998, I was doing more marketing or what I thought was marketing. What I didn't have was a web presence, but my daughter was there to help me. We advertised through flyers, business cards, and finally had a hosted web account on Small Biz. When I look back, I realized how much hard work, time, and money went into ventures that profited me nothing except experience and hard knocks – much like my entire life.

We obtained a small office space near Thomas and 24ᵗʰ Street. I thought I had arrived. I had my own office space. It was upstairs and not ADA-accessible. But, of course, at the time, I did not know anything about ADA-accessibility requirements. We had three rooms and paid $800 a month for an 800-square foot space. It was extremely inexpensive compared to other office spaces, but you get what you paid for. A man stopped by who was all smiles and congenial who sold us an alarm system, which we did not need. This would be the start of my bad credit. When we moved a year later, we had them remove the alarm system; however, they still wanted us to pay for the alarm, that is, honor the fine print on the contract that we hadn't noticed which said the term was for three years. This is one of the reasons it is extremely difficult for people to sell me anything today. Any salesperson gets an extremely hard time from me.

I only did one marketing presentation for the temporary employment. This was the community center where I'd been sent previously by Mr. Wilson. This was my opportunity to get my feet wet, except I almost drowned. I did get several of the students to sign up; however, only one of them showed up at our office to actually seek employment. Of course, I had no assignment in which to place her. We applied for a contract with the City of Phoenix many times, not only temporary employment services, but computer training. I went through a Small Business and Entrepreneurs workshop sponsored by the City of Phoenix. I was always ahead of my time with ideas and goals, but I could not quite focus on one thing to make it work. The young black man who was doing carpet cleaning was more successful than I was. I did not have the knack for finding out what people want and need and then filling that need and/or want. It always seemed so superficial to me, but I would learn that this is exactly what business is. Sometimes it even involves creating a need where none exists and then filling it. The majority of people are like mind-less cattle that seem to fall for anything. My problem is that I want to help them become better than what they are instead of capitalizing on their helpless state. I'm not really a business woman. Let's face it: I am and always will be a writer and teacher at heart.

Even though I had my own office space, I had to still take temporary jobs to feed my family and pay my bills. My children were both working through Mesa Youth Placement during the summer. My son was at an age that he could work full-time. He disappointed me at that time by lying to me. I depended on his paycheck to help me. This didn't happen. My mother was chiding me about having an office space when I had a house note. Neither my mother, nor anyone else in my family (except for Tracee) helped me or even offered to help me financially. They didn't have the vision I had nor did they want to see the vision.

Just when I'm thinking of closing up the shop due to finances, a good-looking, smooth-talker named Tony shows up. I met him while working at Mesa Community College on Brown Road. I was working for the ex-chancellor who was semi-retired. They eventually built a Science & Computer Center that they named after him at the main campus on Southern & Dobson. I tried my best to obtain a teaching position at the college. However, I was told I had to meet with the Dean of the English Dept. He told me I needed a master's degree to teach. So many times I lost out on opportunities because of that doggone piece of paper! I could teach better than many of the professors at ASU, but because I lacked this requirement, they would not even let me demonstrate my ability.

I had purposed to have my own charter school. I used Wilson Academy's information as a boilerplate and was in the process of putting together my application. I needed a board. One of the women who worked there had such an extensive background. I spoke to her and she agreed. I gave her the form to complete. I ascertained a letter of recommendation from the ex-chancellor, my boss, and from Cody Williams who was then one of the council members for the City of Phoenix. I got one from one of my sisters in Christ, Evangelist Arbuckle who I'd helped through her process of getting her master's degree in Social Work. I'd edited many a paper for her. I thought I was on my way. This would be the first time the application was rejected.

Rejection leads to vulnerability which leads to culpability, especially when you're not depending on God. The office at Mesa Community College where I was working was open so that students could notice and see what was going on. I kept my purse in my drawer which wasn't locked. It wasn't until time to go home that I realized my purse was missing. We searched high and low. I realized one of the students had taken it. I did not have credit cards; I had debit cards. I cancelled them; however, someone had charged over $300 at AutoZone in Tucson. They didn't have a pin, but they had my ID and other information. My bank refunded the $300 and they found my purse in the street not far from the school. My ID and personals were never recovered. I had to get a new ID and replace the other needed information. However, as with all losses, some things you never recover.

T had apparently been doing some networking with another student at the college. We exchanged business cards. His field was entertainment. However, he was smart and had ideas about how we could partner to do great things. He had been in films and had made a movie. People said he looked like a younger version of Ron O'Neal and told me he had played him in his own movie. We filed for a trade name for the business to make movies. Nothing ever came of it. He was married. I visited his wife and talked with her. I saw that he was a con artist. Once again, I didn't use wisdom and learned the hard way. He stayed at the office, sometimes living there. He used my skills and abilities and did not give much back in return. Since he owed me money, I confiscated a lot of his supplies. Nothing became of the business. I ended up putting him out.

I had received another student loan to attend Collins College. A friend and sister in Christ, DC was working there teaching Art Design. She was the creator of the Honeystuff Babies. She commissioned me to write a poem for her, which I did. I was amazed how creative she was. I dabbled into computer design, could use Dreamweaver to create my own website, learned to use Adobe Photoshop, and the language of HTML. However, everything I created was "Mickey Mouse" compared to her. We should always stick to what we're good at doing. The key is to find your forte and make it work for you. DC had something else I didn't have: she was light-skinned and a bit younger. She also used more wisdom than I did at that time. She, like most of my friends, was someone with whom I prayed. We prayed for God to send us God-fearing good men as husbands. She, like most of my friends, got married. I did not. In fact, she married a younger man whose parents won the lottery in Chicago.

I learned a great deal at Collins College and could design my own website for my business. We dabbled into temporary employment and applied for various grants and contracts. We received none. F.A.I.T.H. Ministries (nonprofit) and Geri Lorraine Enterprises (for profit) were both born out of F.A.I.T.H. Services (no profit). I had no middle name because my mother thought I was going to be a boy and had planned to name me Jerry. When I was born a girl, she decided to name me Geri Lorraine. I was told my father didn't like that, so she dropped the "Geri" and I got no middle name. So, I liked the name and decided to use it for my business later in life.

I couldn't maintain everything financially. We closed the office; however, I was having trouble with my homeowner's association. I owed a little over $500, but because, when I went to court I told him I was not able to pay it and was not going to at that time, he, being a part-time fill-in trial judge and attorney, decided to teach me a lesson. I never got my day in court; they saw to that. I was railroaded and ended up having to pay over $3,000 – which included their court fees. So much for the money I'd received from my student loans. What makes matters worse is that this happened to me twice. I went through so much just to keep a roof over my children's heads, keep our home, and not have to pay rent to anyone. Bankruptcy was a nemesis that would haunt me the rest of my life, it seemed.

Finally, I ended up at a school which would be the last charter school for which I would work: Genesis Academy in Phoenix. I first saw the ad on the Arizona Dept. of Education's online job board. I called and Karen. who was the director scheduled me for an interview. When I got there, I felt immediately at home.

I met two women, one of whom as a black woman who I'd met at the charter school run by the woman in charge of the Birthing Project. I talked with Karen who immediately hired me. She had lost her English teacher a few months before the end of the school year. I would learn later why. I was introduced to the Education Specialist, Paul. I found him pleasant, matter-of-fact, and knowledgeable.

Just as with all places I'd worked, I did everything to the glory of God. I worked hard. I encountered opposition at first from the students because I'm more of a disciplinarian, but before long, they realized I wasn't going anywhere, and they let up. Eventually, they saw that I cared whether or not they learned anything. The population was mostly Hispanic, although the school was multicultural, like the staff. I was the only other black teacher, however. I was hired during the same time as an overweight, blonde, white woman, who I interacted with, mostly because we were both women, lived in Mesa, and started to carpool. She was extremely intelligent and Science and Math were her specialties. I taught English and then later Math.

When I look back, I remember at times doing the job of 3 people, giving of myself, my time, my energy, my talents and gifts to the school. The money was pretty good and we received bonuses. This is the only reason I stayed for just about 3 years. Otherwise, I would have left long before. I discovered that the director, although tall, blonde, and white – what the world seems to think is the standard of beauty – was really a devil in disguise. PS tried to warn me of this, but of course, I didn't listen to him. I was targeted for his job when Karen and her sidekick, managed to get everyone to turn against him. I discovered that her sidekick was dumb like a fox. Paul was promised things that never came to pass. I felt so sorry that I had penned my name to a petition that Karen's sidekick had passed around.

I remember one time that Karen blew up at me in a meeting with the black woman and her sidekick. Her venom was so great that my period started. I found her to be a person who knew how to manipulate everyone and everything around her. She seemed at first to be a likable person. She even professed to be a Christian. She was actually evil and conniving. However, I cannot put all the blame on her. I made mistakes and did not trust God. I let the casino take away a great deal of my financial resources. Mostly, I discovered that no matter how hard I worked, no matter what I accomplished, no matter how valuable my services were initially, every employer used me without mercy. Then, when I made one mistake, or proved that I was human, I was told that everything I did prior was of no effect. All my good had been erased. This is when I knew that they saw me as a usable and expendable commodity. I, the black woman, was not a person. I was a thing. I was still the "house n--." This was all I was ever going to be. It was this resentment that led to my disassociation with them. I left Genesis, in mind and spirit and had lined up another job (my last job) two weeks prior to them telling me that I would not be coming back. It still hurt because of everything that I had done for them, but I eventually tried to leave somewhat on good terms through a termination and goodbye letter.

I interviewed for and landed a job with Gila River Indian Community Juvenile Detention Center in Sacaton, Arizona. The organization has now gone through tremendous re-organization and changes and the name "Rehabilitation" has replaced "Detention." There is one director over both the adult and the juvenile facilities.

However, when I was hired, I was interviewed by Nancy, who I first thought was a male. Although I never asked her, and she never said so directly, I heard her mention several times about her "partner." I believed she was a homosexual and she claimed to be Christian. Since this had nothing whatsoever to do with my job and her as my employer, I never addressed it. Even though things were far from perfect, as people are far from perfect, she was a better boss than Karen.

I was hired as the Detention Education Teacher and had to be certified for the position. Another teacher was hired who I thought was pretty congenial. I can still see her smiling face. She was a good person, but she could not get over the fact that she and I were treated like second class citizens and the two teacher's assistants were treated as though they were the actual teachers. We were housed in the "dungeon" as I call it – the small facility that used to be the only facility until they built the bigger one around it. The detention center seemed more of a country club for the Native Americans. They ate well, had a roof over their heads, and had a nice basketball court, volleyball net on sand, green grass where they got to play kickball, soccer, and football. They even had a recreation center with ping pong tables, TV and video games, board games, and exercise equipment. They had education classes. The security guards were more babysitters than anything else. There were times when a few of the residents, as they were called, were unruly or disobeyed the rules and had to be put in the individual cells. What was so strange is that sometimes particular residents wanted to be put in the cells. They said this was so they could think and be to themselves. Sometimes it was because they wanted to avoid certain activities and to go to sleep.

I could devote a whole book to just this one experience, but I won't at this time. In a nutshell, out of necessity, I eventually "earned" the right to have a classroom in the "big house." The other teacher had been let go at the same time she had decided she didn't want to work there. Apparently, she didn't get along with the other teacher's aides. In addition, she and Nancy had words where she basically called Nancy a liar. Of course, this is what the teacher told me. I remember feeling a sense of dread when I saw Nancy and the person in charge of Security going down the corridor. I knew what was about to happen. The next thing I saw was the three of them heading down the hallway. The teacher told me it was nice working with me and "goodbye." This reminded me of when I left Genesis. I told them it was nice working with them and "goodbye."

The students tried to be difficult and tried their best not to like me, but eventually they too saw that I cared about them, and they loved me after that. I keep remembering a saying I saw somewhere: "children don't care how much you know until they know how much you care." This is so true. The only degree they cared about was the degree to which I taught them and took time with them to help them learn.

I had just come from working at a charter school with close to 30 students in a classroom. Having a class of 5 to 7 students was a blessing in and of itself. I was making over $50,000 a year. At Genesis we had to have on business attire with students who were sagging pants, t-shirts, and tennis shoes. My uniform at JDRC (as it was called then) was a pair of jeans, tennis shoes, and short-sleeved shirts with the Gila River Indian Community and detention center patch. I loved those students. They were my "loveable little criminals." I would purposely not look at the incoming information on them so as not to prejudice myself against them. They had broken the law, but they were still my students. My job was to teach them to the best of my ability. Usually, it was during the weekly counseling sessions that I discovered they had committed armed robbery, physical assault, sexual assault, molestation, truancy, and a few times, murder. Yes, they had broken the law, but they were still children. All of the faculty members were God-fearing people. We had prayer sessions in the mornings in the teacher's break room. This was truly a blessing. I learned a lot. I gave a lot. I experienced racism, insults, and treated unfair many times. This was from management. I had fun. I laughed, went on field trips, and enjoyed games with the staff and students. These are all experiences I would not have missed for the world.

My mother and my uncle (mother's sister's husband) were stricken with cancer. Against my pleadings and advice, they both opted for chemo. My uncle's tumor was inoperable but he was treated with radiation and chemo. My mother had the operation and chemo treatments. I went on part-time family leave. My father was there to help her and my aunt was there to help my uncle. I brought my mother home the lunch I received from the school every day. There were a few times she needed me to take her to the doctor and I picked her up. A few times I picked up her prescriptions for her. I later discovered that she felt I should have done more for her, even though my father was there and helped her. However, she never told me this at the time.

I used this opportunity to work on the grant for the school for which God gave me a vision many years prior. For some reason, I just knew God was going to bless me. Without faith it's impossible to please God. I knew my faith was being tested in so many areas. Lighthouse Publishing had re-published my book, The Last Visitor, in paperback. My uncle never got a chance to read it. He did not survive the cancer treatments. I was so angry. I remember being at the birthday party they had for both of my uncles: my mother's brother and him. Their birthday was on the same day. The doctor who was "treating" my uncle had also been invited. My aunt introduced him to everyone as if he were a celebrity. I saw him as a hired killer. I believe in natural healing with herbs. God has given us everything on this green earth to cure all of our ills, but most of society prefers drugs because we refuse to live with any type of pain, physical or emotional. The main character in my story also died of cancer. My cousin, my uncle's daughter who loved to read and had bought a copy of the book, commented to me months later after my uncle's death: "Lorraine, that book..."and she never finished her sentence. Her smile disappeared and she grew silent. I could tell she was remembering her father's death.

I applied for the grant. What ensued afterwards was nothing short of miraculous. We, along with several other programs, were asked to do a revision. We were among two other new programs who had never submitted a proposal before. It was one of the hardest, most intense, and longest grants I have ever had to put together. The other programs should have been "old hat" at the process; however, we all were invited to a two-day training session. My daughter attended the first day with me, but I was on my own the second day. We received the grant!

After the first session of classes, I realized that I could not work part-time or full-time at another job and still have a successful adult education program. There was just too much work, too many reports, and I had to wear so many different hats. Through prayer I realized that it was time to step out on faith. I gave my notice at Gila River Indian Community. They scheduled one of our graduations during that time. I was the keynote speaker for the second time. One of the graduates wanted me to sing. I wanted so badly to sing "I Believe" by Fantasia Morino, which is what I did — very badly, even with the accompaniment tape. Oh well, I had fun, and I was never going to see them again if I didn't want to do so.

Working for Family & Freedom

I vowed that I would never work for anyone else again. I asked God to make this happen for me. God has opened so many doors for me. I struggle and I don't make a great deal of money. Yes, at times I feel the pangs of not receiving a check for over $2,000 every two weeks. Yes, my mother and other family members (except my daughter) think it was the dumbest move I ever made. However, I am happier than I have ever been. I know God is with me. Also, God has told me: "If you want to have money, don't go to the casino." It is only when I disobey in this area that I have problems. Yes, I owe over $130,000 in student loans, mostly due to interest over the many years and several deferments. Yes, I was audited by the IRS and owe them over $8,000. However, I have purposed in my heart that if I don't earn enough to pay all of this back, or if it is not wiped away miraculously, I will have to take a vow of poverty. The only time I am resentful and angry is when I remember how the black race has never received reparations. I remember how my ancestors were enslaved, raped, lynched, murdered, burned, shot, ridiculed, ostracized, dehumanized, and stripped of heritage, identity, homeland, and dignity, both during and after slavery. I remember how most of the whites now enjoy the fruits of what lynching, murder, slavery, and rape have wrought in this country. Even our so-called first black president cares nothing about seeing that we get reparations. He is the champion for Native Americans and homosexuals.

I am so devastated that black people must be content with having two slabs of stone carved inside of the state capitol. They are not mentioned individually. They have no names, no identity, and their descendants are still in degradation, dehumanization, and poverty. Dr. Martin Luther King took us as far as he could take us. We need leaders who will take us even farther. Unfortunately, Barrack Obama is not that person. He is one of those who have "identified with the oppressor." I remember the young female who exclaimed on national TV right after Obama was elected, *"All right, now we're gonna get reparations!"* I wanted to cry even then. Lately, I've heard another black woman say with a sigh, *"I'm so tired of trying to defend him."* From my perspective, reparations for black people should have been first on his agenda, not health care so people can access more drugs to make the big pharmaceutical companies wealthy.

So now I work in my own business, Geri Lorraine Enterprises, LLC providing business consulting to individuals and organizations. We were DBE certified many years ago and have had several clients, helping them start their non-profit organizations, getting their 501(c)3, and procuring grants for them. One of my clients was Calais Campbell, one of the Arizona Diamondbacks. We had to do an entire re-organization for him and create the CRC Foundation, Inc. in Chandler, Arizona. CRC Foundation provides outreach activities to youth and offers several scholarships. In addition, I rely on pennies from the small grants we receive and the books I'm continuing to write and publish through FM Publishing Co.

Freedom can be achieved but always comes with a price. It's a matter of priorities. I've worked since I was nine years old: from babysitting to business consulting. I've made little and I've made more (never a lot). My daughter, Tracee is the Managing Director for Geri Lorraine Enterprises, LLC and the president of one of its subsidiaries. She creates specialized and personalized greeting cards and distributes different types of office supplies. I have staff of 4 people who run the nonprofit office for me; my daughter Tracee, serves faithfully as the Program Director and also as the Secretary/Treasurer of the Board of Directors. She's diligent, intelligent, creative, and seeking a degree at CAC through online classes. We offer GED classes and rental/mortgage and utility assistance to the community. We have WNTBS (What Needs To Be Said) Internet Radio and Newspaper. We've even started Casa Grande Chess Club. We have a certified tutor online course. I'm able to offer bible studies and workshops, counseling, employment services, financial workshops, and serve the community. Yes, despite everything, I am still a servant, but no longer a slave.

Do We Really Retire?

"Retirement: It's nice to get out of the rat race, but you have to learn to get along with less cheese." (Gene Perret)

Most of us work 50 to 55 years and finally reach this stage. Do we really retire, or do we just wait to die?

There is a chapter in the book, *How Do You Retire When You Are Unemployed?* This chapter discusses a PBS documentary conducted by filmmaker Marian Marzynski called *My Retirement Dreams*, where Marzynski explored a Miami Beach retirement community. According to Marzynski, most of the residents reported that "some were bored, some were physically inactive, some were expanding their minds, and many were waiting for destiny to show them the way." Friedrich Nietzche said, *"Is not life a hundred times too short for us to bore ourselves?"* Marzyski pointed out that what makes for a happy retirement has little to do with your age, education, or your level of income. What a contrast to all of the retirement financial planning advertisements like "how to be rich when you retire," or "help increase your retirement income and guarantee it lasts a lifetime."

I remember playing *The Game of Life* as a child. It was originally created in 1860 by Milton Bradley as *The Checked Game of Life*. The game simulates a person's travels through his or her life, from college to retirement, with jobs, marriages and children (or not) along the way. Two to six players can participate in one game; however, variations of the game have been made to accommodate a maximum of eight or ten players. The modern version was originally published one hundred years later, in 1960 (then "heartily endorsed" by Art

Linkletter, with a circular picture of him on the box) by the Milton Bradley Company (now a subsidiary of Hasbro). We played it with my parents. I even used it as an instructional tool for the residents at the juvenile detention center. The game is exciting, eye-opening, and fun – not at all like the cruel reality of life, but it did make you do some critical thinking about your choices. You still could make choices but the chance roll of the dice is what determined how far ahead you moved and where you landed each time. The male pieces were blue and the female pieces were pink. I'm sure they're revising this game as I write this. You could choose to take the route to get married and have children or not. When it came to deciding on a career, the roll of the dice decided for you. What is amazing is how the game contents changed over the years. It tells you a great deal about real life and our society. The 1970's/1980's version included Salaries, Share the Wealth cards, Life Events, Insurance and Stock, Lucky Day, and Retirement.

The 1991 version had changed it to Careers and Salaries, Types of Spaces, Occupation Spaces, and added LIFE Tiles, Buying a House, but kept the Insurance and Stock, and Retirement. Then came the CD-ROM version. It included "Life's Little Games." This version included chance cards with different names such as Safe Cracker, Up or Down, Get a Life, Treasure Chest, Skunk Money, Cannonball, Crane Dump, and Trash Can. With these cards you could take money from your opponents by getting "revenge" or other means. It included a flavor of office politics, wheeling and dealing, and gambling like slot games found at the casino.

In 2000, they released the 40th anniversary edition with virtually no changes. An updated version of the game's 1992 format was released in 2005 with a few game play changes. The new *Game of Life* was more realistic and tried to add in extra elements to reduce chance, although it is still primarily chance based and still rewards players for taking risks. The person who opted for college started with $100,000 in debt instead of $40,000 in debt as in the previous 1992 version. This version also came with special career renovations. A person could only get the lower wage cards as a starting salary. They also added special attributes to the careers. However, all of the amounts, including money on the tiles and chance cards increased (inflation). The current version separates the careers where no degree is required: Salesperson, Hair Stylist, Mechanic, Police Officer, Entertainer, and Athlete; and those that require a degree: Teacher, Computer Designer, Accountant, Veterinarian, Doctor, and Lawyer.

There have been several criticisms of the game where it has been noted that luck plays too large a role in determining the winner of the game, with Life Cards, which are essentially random, being the prime determinant of the winner. These critics feel that aspects of the game where a user has to make a decision, such as attending college or purchasing insurance, have a very small effect in the outcome. I think Milton and Art were on the right track. It's a great deal like life, especially today. What's interesting is that from 1860 to present, the components in the game that have remained are working and retirement.

* * * * *

"There's one thing I've always wanted to do before I quit: RETIRE" (Groucho Marx)

* * * * *

My goal was to retire at the age of 55, which I will achieve (if I live long enough) in the year 2011. What do people mean when they say they want to retire? I believe they mean they want to stop working so hard, so many hours, and just do what they want to do with their time. The problem is by the time most people retire, they are just plain "tired." Sometimes they are able to do something else, provided they have enough retirement money and/or savings, like travel, work on a hobby, their garden, their old cars, their homes, knitting, golfing, etc. However, some of them end up raising their grandchildren, taking a part-time job, volunteering to keep busy and active in the community, or living from one doctor visit to the next. There is an old saying, *"People spend the first half of their lives losing their health trying to get wealthy, and then they spend the last half of their lives losing their wealth trying to get healthy again."* I am not one of those people. It's been 13 years since I've taken any kind of prescription drugs. I haven't visited the doctor in 3 years. I want to die on God's timetable and in the best health I can.

Unemployed Doesn't Mean Unemployable

"An 'acceptable' level of unemployment means that the government economist to whom it is acceptable still has a job." (Author unknown)

Currently, there is a 9.5% unemployment rate in the U.S., a 9.6% unemployment rate in the State of Arizona, the same as that of the United States average, and 11.6% unemployment rate in Pinal County, where I reside. Congress just passed a bill that they had slowly deliberated over, to continue unemployment benefits to those who are still without jobs. Those who were smart enough to continue to file their weekly claims even though they received no benefits for 5 continuous weeks finally received retroactive benefits.

Our country has been outsourcing every type of employment they can think of. Outsourcing refers to a company which contracts with another company to provide services that otherwise might be performed by in-house employees. Many large companies now outsource jobs such as call center services, e-mail services, and payroll. These jobs are handled by separate companies that specialize in each service, and are often located overseas. There are many reasons that companies outsource various jobs, but the most prominent advantage seems to be the fact that it often saves money. Many of the companies that provide outsourcing services are able to do the work for considerably less money, as they don't have to provide benefits to their workers and have fewer overhead expenses to worry about. WNS is a business that claims to be "experts" in delivering business solutions and advertises to help businesses "extend your enterprise."

On one hand it may seem to make good business sense to outsource. This helps them to save on overhead especially with regard to personnel. The issue I have is that the outsourcing is done to other countries instead of within the U.S. Everything we have is made in China. I remember a time when everyone thought something made in China was an inferior product - a product to be shunned. Not so today. We have big corporations who have to make money, they say, to show a profit to all of their wonderful stockholders, who, by the way, are the only ones who are making any money.

An article was published by the DRUM Major Institute for Public Policy called "The Impact of Outsourcing on the American Worker." This article was written 7 years ago, May 2, 2003. In the article, Ernie Nounou offers three key solutions: 1) lower payroll taxes to reduce the burden on companies and make hiring employees a more attractive option; 2) reduce the burden of companies to have to provide health insurance to employees; 3) put a stop to visa abuse whereby companies import lower wage workers that puts the American worker at a disadvantage in the competitive job market. Seven years later, after Bush and now Obama, we have a higher payroll tax, the Healthcare Bill that mandates that everyone must have health insurance (same type of scam as requiring everyone to have car insurance), and not only continued importation of lower wage workers, but a lawsuit filed against the State of Arizona because the State has tried to strengthen the federal law that prevents illegal immigrants from residing in and working in the U.S. They say there is wisdom in listening to wise counsel; however, we have shown ourselves to be unwise.

In June, 2010, there was an article published on the web by Money & Company called "Is there no solving the U.S. unemployment problem?" Two important points from this article:

> "The Bureau of Labor Statistics projects that seven of the 10 employment sectors that will see the largest gains over the next decade won't require much more than some on-the-job training. These include home healthcare aides, customer service representatives and food preparers and servers. 'People with bachelor's degrees will increasingly get not very highly satisfactory jobs,' said W. Norton Grubb, a professor at UC Berkeley's School of Education. 'In that sense, people are getting more schooling than jobs are available."

> "On Fortune magazine's website this week Ford wrote: As technology continues to accelerate, the number and types of jobs that can be automated is certain to expand dramatically. It's not just factory workers that can be replaced by robots and machines: Rapidly improving software automation and specialized artificial intelligence applications will make knowledge worker and professional occupations requiring college educations and advanced skills increasingly vulnerable."

Amazingly, this article drew only 28 comments. I have listed a few of them below:

"This is clearly not just a government problem. This week the auto industry said it's going to shop more work to Mexico. Corporations are unwilling to part with any profit to hiring workers. People will be looking for jobs for a long time to come. I've been listening to great job searching advice on an Internet radio show at www.jobtalkamerica.com" **Posted by: sam | June 12, 2010 at 11:16 AM**

"Part of the problem is a poorly educated workforce. In our public schools, if you leave aside the top 10% of students, the lack of ambition and the lack of educational quality is remarkable. Look at the results of the California Standards Test and the National Assessment of Educational Progress, or the TIMMS. Dismal. The result is that most of our high school graduates are unqualified for high-skill jobs. We have to import high-skill workers from overseas. And when we can't, those jobs are going begging while millions of Americans languish in long-term structural unemployment." **Posted by: Schigolch | June 12, 2010 at 11:45 AM**

"A short history of radical ideas that caused outrage and controversy but ultimately were very good for the economy and jobs. Radical idea 1) Free and mandatory primary school education for children. (Wow, did this raise a few eyebrows and and few tempers.) Turned out to be a pretty good idea, though. Radical idea 2) Much later : Free and mandatory high school education. (What a waste! History and *geography? No way!) In the end, time showed that this was a pretty good idea. Radical idea 3) The outrage over this one was tremendous. It occurred to someone that young adults in post-secondary education were, in fact, adults. So, a long time ago in 2011, someone suggested paying university students a living wage to attend university - with the scholarships based on the future hiring needs that businesses were projecting in their business plans. And just like any job : Daily Attendance Not Optional. We all know now that this idea - almost instantly - stopped young people from dropping out of high school, kept young people from competing for jobs before they were ready, created demand for housing and cost almost nothing. The young people had been collecting various cash benefits anyway. Not only that, young people started graduating with no outstanding debt. This gave them a solid economic base to work from as the started their careers and their young families. Soon enough, many of them could afford to buy a home. Conclusion : Advances in technology are about to make it very inexpensive to create and deliver quality educational materials.*

Much of the controversy about the "job" market is - in fact - revolving around the fact that the educational system needs to be upgraded again? The tricky part right now is that people in post-secondary education are adults. They need money to live their lives. Asking them to pay (instead of paying them) is ridiculous? But it's only 2010. Wait until

you hear the outrage when this idea is implemented. And if that history course I took (that was so controversial in 1900) is any teacher - the idea will, indeed, be implemented soon. In any case - it's a nice thought? May all beneficial wishes come true in beneficial ways! Namke von Federlein"
Posted by: Namke von Federlein | June 12, 2010 at 10:00 PM

"There is a solution to the U.S. unemployment problem: Put in place radical policies that encourage Americans to make what they buy. If the United States doesn't start producing what it consumes – as it did for hundreds of years – then a dismal future awaits. It doesn't matter if a foreign company makes it – cell phones, flat panel TVs or laptops – so long as there are American workers making the hundreds of billions of dollars of products that are now made offshore. Even dental floss is made in China, how stupid is that! Despite the yap about automation and robotics reducing the need for workers, manufacturing creates a huge number of jobs off the factory floor – in design, research, software, logistics, in the supply chain for components and materials, energy, accounting and legal. For generations of America, manufacturing created the wealth of the country, which translated into taxes, which translated into a high standard of living and jobs for teachers, librarians, policemen, politicians, soldiers and 22 million bureaucrats. Without industry the U.S. has withered. How is the country going to pay for the retirement of a the largest *generation in history by creating jobs as dental hygenists?"* **Posted by: Richard McCormack | June 13, 2010 at 07:00 AM**

">>'People with bachelor's degrees will increasingly get not very highly satisfactory jobs,<<'And people with law degrees, masters degrees, and PhDs should expect even less satisfaction, especially when the $1,300/month student loan bills come due. Yup, Welcome to America, Home of the Smartest Poor People on The Planet." **Posted by: Adam Negrete | June 13, 2010 at 07:17 AM**

Obviously, our country has started down a road from which it will not recover. However, one need only check the political pulse of history up to today and you will find that all of this has been carefully orchestrated by the elite who own the government. They know that this economy will fail. They know that the U.S. will crumble. They have planned everything carefully to usher in and achieve the New World Order. When there are no more jobs and people cannot support themselves but, of course, they still have basic needs, what happens? Why the government supports them, of course – socialism at its best. Of course, when the government gives you everything you need to sustain your very life you have also given them control of your very life—from the food you eat, the water you drink, and the air you breathe. They will tell you where you can go, what you can see, what you can see, and what you will do. This is what they have wanted all along: control. How best to achieve such by corrupting and running the economy? You may have to "make sacrifices" as Obama has stated, but you can rest assured that the elite will make no such sacrifices. Someone said that we will not recognize America in

2012. They are correct. In fact, it will no longer be called the U.S. or America. The Constitution will be rendered "null and void," for purely security reasons of course. The system that we all feared will "rear its ugly head" and the "man of perdition" and "the number of his name" will be revealed.

Those who are unemployed will not have to worry. They will still be employable. Yes, those of us who owe student loans, owe government taxes, and have debts due to creditors; they will put us to work. We will work for free, that is, become "indentured servants." Sound familiar? We will have two choices: work for them and give allegiance to their world order, that is, their government and their system (the mark of the antichrist) or go to prison. Later, the option of prison will seem too easy; it will be replaced with "lose your life."

The Best Employer

"God is the one great employer, thinker, planner, supervisor." (Anonymous)

I say work while it is still day as the Bible says. There comes a time when no man will work. Only what you do for God (Yah) will last. Everything else will vanish away and wither as the green grass. The fact that work and lack thereof is such a big issue due to unemployment is interesting considering the fact that God (Yah) says,

> *"Remember the Sabbath day and keep it holy. Six days you labor and do all your work but the seventh day is the Sabbath day of the Lord. You shall not do any work, neither you, your household, including your servants, your animals, and the stranger that is within your gates. For in six days the Lord God (Yahweh) created the heavens and the earth and all that in them is, and he rested the seventh day and hallowed it"* (Exodus 20:9-16).

We live in a country where Black Hebrew Israelites do not know who they are and have been lied to and deceived for years. In so doing, they give allegiance to traditional Christianity and Catholicism that supports paganism which includes celebration of Christmas and Easter. In addition, this system holds Sunday as the "Lord's Day." As the disciples said, *"We ought to obey God [Yah] rather than man."* (Acts 5:29) For everything God (Yah) has, the Devil has a counterfeit. When will people shake the sleep out of their spiritual eyes?

138

I submit that the true believers should accept God's (Yah's) offer of employment. He has your resume and you don't need references. His compensation and benefits come through a variety of sources and means. David, the psalmist said, *"I was young and now old, but I've never seen the righteous forsaken nor his seed begging bread."* (Psalm 37:35) God (Yah) always provides for his workers. He is faithful and He is just. He gives you one day off each week to rest, to meet with him, and have total fellowship with Him and other workers so He can strengthen His relationship with you. He gives you peace, comfort, and reassurance through the Comforter, the Holy Spirit. He sacrificed all for you through his son, Jesus (Yahoshua) so that after all your work is done you can retire from this earthly realm and reign with Him throughout eternity. The Bible says,

> *"Eyes have not seen, ears have not heard, nor entered into the heart of man the things that God [Yah] has prepared for those that love Him."* (1 Corinthian 2:9)

Jesus (Yahoshua) said,

> *"In my Father's house are many mansions. If it were not so, I would have told you. I go to prepare a place for you, and if I go to prepare a place for you, I will come again and receive you unto myself, so that where I am, there you may be also."* (John 14:2)

We should focus on these things when we weigh our choices in serving the antichrist and his system of evil and enmity against God, or staying true to Yah's word. The apostle Paul said,

"But what things were gain to me, those I counted loss for Christ [Yahoshua]. Yea doubtless, and I count all things but loss for the excellency of the knowledge of Christ Jesus [Yahoshua] my Lord: for whom I have suffered the loss of all things, and do count them but dung, that I may win Christ [Yahoshua], And be found in him, not having mine own righteousness, which is of the law, but that which is through the faith of Christ [Yahoshua], the righteousness which is of God [Yah] by faith: That I may know him, and the power of his resurrection, and the fellowship of his sufferings, being made conformable unto his death ... Brethren, I count not myself to have apprehended: but this one thing I do, forgetting those things which are behind, and reaching forth unto those things which are before, I press toward the mark for the prize of the high calling of God [Yah] in Christ Jesus [Yahoshua]." (Philippians 3:7-14)

Yes, I work for the kingdom of God (Yah). I am still and will forever be His servant, but never a slave to sin, but a servant of righteousness. When my work is done in this earthly realm, I want to hear my employer say,

"Well done good and faithful servant. You have been faithful over a few things, I will make you ruler over many things: enter you into the joy of your Lord [Yah]." (Matthew 25:21)

Now that is what I call the best retirement!

About The Author

Dr. Elizabeth A. James (E.A. James) has been writing for over 40 years. She is a licensed and ordained minister and has been President and Founder of Fast And Indispensable Temporary Help (F.A.I.T.H.) Ministries, Inc. since February, 1999. She is also the Editor-in-Chief of FM Publishing Company (2009) and Senior Managing Director of Geri Lorraine Enterprises, LLC (2000). In 2014, she became a supplier, independent marketer, and supporter with TAG Team Marketing International and a dedicated member of the Black Business Network.

After attending over 10 colleges, she has a doctorate in Theology & Biblical Counseling, a master's in Education, bachelor's degree in English, and major course work in subjects such as Business Management, Biomedical Engineering, Pre-Med, and Chemistry.

In addition to many other accomplishments, E.A. James has received the Woman of Excellence Award, is a member of blackwritersconnect.com, and has won several awards for her poetry. She is currently a business consultant, certified teacher, and a Nationally-Certified Manager of Program Improvement.

Titles by E.A. James:

Spiritual Cosmetics for the Soul (devotionals)
The Last Visitor (historical fiction)
Being a Well Body of Believers (nonfiction)
This Hill I Climb (poetry)
The Reason Why I Sing (poetry/songs)
Driving Tips for BOOHs (Bats Out of Hell) (satire)
7-Day Emergency Help for OWIACs (Of Whom I Am Chief) (devotionals)
Why I Should Hate Men, But Don't (nonfiction)
Will Work for Food, Family & Freedom (nonfiction)
Casino Con: An Eye-Opening Look From the Inside Out (nonfiction)

Publication and Catalog Ordering Information

To get other books by E.A. James or to inquire about screenplay production rights:

FM Publishing Company
P.O. Box 215
Cherokee, NC 28719

Website: www.fmpublishingcompany.com

Email: fmpublishing@cox.net

Fax: 800-518-1219

FM Publishing Co.

* 9 7 8 1 9 3 1 6 7 1 0 6 4 *